S0-AGD-471

# HOW TO THROW

## THE

# Ultimate

# SLUMBER
# PARTY

— JAMIE KYLE McGILLIAN —

**STERLING CHILDREN'S BOOKS**
New York

*For Bailey and Devan, my little party girls.*

## STERLING CHILDREN'S BOOKS
New York

An Imprint of Sterling Publishing Co., Inc.
1166 Avenue of the Americas
New York, NY 10036

STERLING CHILDREN'S BOOKS and the distinctive Sterling Children's Books logo
are registered trademarks of Sterling Publishing Co., Inc.

Text © 2010, 2017 Jamie Kyle McGillian
Illustrations © 2017 Sterling Publishing Co., Inc.

All rights reserved. No part of this publication may be reproduced, stored in a retrieval system,
or transmitted in any form or by any means (including electronic, mechanical, photocopying,
recording, or otherwise) without prior written permission from the publisher.

ISBN 978-1-4549-2519-4

Library of Congress Cataloging-in-Publication Data

McGillian, Jamie Kyle.
  Sleepover party! : Games and giggles for a fun night / Jamie Kyle McGillian.
    p. cm.
  Includes index.
  ISBN-13: 978-1-4027-2978-2
  ISBN-10: 1-4027-2978-2
  1.  Sleepovers—Juvenile literature. 2.  Children's parties—Juvenile literature.  I.  Title.

GV1205.M33 2007
793.2'1—dc22

                                        2006029509


Distributed in Canada by Sterling Publishing Co., Inc.
c/o Canadian Manda Group, 664 Annette Street
Toronto, Ontario, Canada M6S 2C8
Distributed in the United Kingdom by GMC Distribution Services
Castle Place, 166 High Street, Lewes, East Sussex, England BN7 1XU
Distributed in Australia by NewSouth Books
45 Beach Street, Coogee, NSW 2034, Australia

For information about custom editions, special sales, and premium and corporate
purchases, please contact Sterling Special Sales at 800-805-5489 or specialsales@
sterlingpublishing.com.

Manufactured in China

Lot #:
2   4   6   8   10   9   7   5   3   1
06/17

sterlingpublishing.com

Illustrations by Kristin Logsdon
Cover and interior design by Ryan Thomman

# Contents

# INTRODUCTION

## IT'S YOUR PARTY!

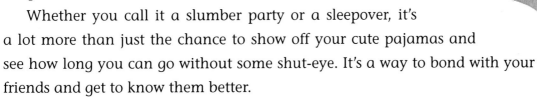

What's more fun than a party with all your friends? A *slumber* party with all your friends! Invite the gang over to chat, laugh, play, sing, munch, and dance the night away. In the morning, you may be a little short on sleep, but it'll be worth it.

Whether you call it a slumber party or a sleepover, it's a lot more than just the chance to show off your cute pajamas and see how long you can go without some shut-eye. It's a way to bond with your friends and get to know them better.

So kick back and have fun! Tell your friends about your latest crush and see what they think. Do some palm reading. Get your nails done. Send shivers down each other's spine with a scary story. Learn how to do something you've never done before. Or just act silly. It's all up to you, because it's your party!

This book is filled with ideas to make your sleepover creative, memorable, and lots of fun. So, come on—let's start planning!

# CHAPTER 1

# PARTY PLANNER: THAT'S YOU!

"Lindsay had a beach party sleepover. It was awesome. Everyone wore sunglasses and bathing suits and had colored zinc oxide on their noses. We painted a giant beach scene and hung it on the wall. Then we played games with beach balls. We drank frozen juice drinks and ate sandwiches on a beach blanket. In the morning, my face hurt from smiling too much!"

—Ali, 12, on her first sleepover

Sleepovers, slumber parties, pajama parties—
what do you call them?

  "I call them stay-up-overs!"
—Jackie, 10

Sleepovers aren't just for birthdays—anytime is the right time to party!

Think about what kind of party you would like to have. Will there be a theme? Do you want to play loud music? Do you and your friends want to dance and sing? Will you and your friends dress up? Or, can you see them chilling at your dinner table in their shorts and T-shirts? Will dinner be served? What kind of food do you want to have? Can you imagine doing craft projects or baking? What about a guest entertainer? Would a family member or friend be willing to teach your friends Irish step dancing, sign language, or knitting? Who knew there was so much to think about and plan for? But don't worry—asking these questions is the first step to throwing an awesome slumber party.

## GETTING PERMISSION

The first thing you should do is have a conversation with your parents. If they give you permission to host a party, talk with them about any concerns they may have. Ask them how many friends you can invite, what time they can come over, where you'll all sleep, etc. Then make a guest list and run it by your parents. This would also be a good time to discuss if your party will be co-ed (meaning that both boys and girls will be invited).

## WHAT'S YOUR DREAM PARTY?

Get ready to brainstorm. Take out a pen and some paper (or take out your writing tablet if you have one) and get ready to make some lists. Writing things down will help you organize ideas and also keep track of details once your plans start to solidify.

The first list you'll want to make is a list of potential party themes (that is, if you decide to have a theme at all—it's up to you!). In order to do this, think about what interests you. What kind of music do you like? What are your favorite books? These are great questions to get the brain juices flowing. Next, ask yourself what kind of party *you* would enjoy attending, and what that might look like. Do you imagine a totally transformed living room, or just a few simple decorations? Think outside the box! Your theme could be anything, from *Star Wars* to Taylor Swift look-alikes to a zombie bash. If you're really struggling to think of original themes, turn to page 18 for inspiration.

Once your list is complete, review your options and decide which ideas you really love. Keep narrowing down your options until you find the one theme that perfectly suits you.

## LISTS, LISTS, AND MORE LISTS!

After you've chosen a theme, the listing doesn't stop! You may also find it helpful to make some to-do lists. A to-do list helps you understand how big or small your tasks are, and also helps you stay focused and on top of things. Plus, it's very satisfying when you can check items off your list! When you are organized, you can accomplish a lot. Here are three examples of to-do lists to tackle at the beginning, middle, and end of your planning process:

### Two to Three Weeks Before the Party
- ❑ Discuss party plans with a parent.
- ❑ Make a guest list.
- ❑ Make invitations and send them out.
- ❑ Plan the menu.
- ❑ Pick the theme and think of decorations to match.

### One Week Before the Party
- ❑ Buy paper plates, plasticware, and decorations.
- ❑ Write a shopping list for food and drinks.
- ❑ Decide what to put in the goodie bags.
- ❑ Make awesome playlists.
- ❑ Check that all guests have responded.

### Day Before or Day of the Party
- ❑ Clean the house.
- ❑ Get out your sleeping bag.
- ❑ Shop for the food and drinks.

- ☐ Hang party decorations.
- ☐ Blow up balloons.
- ☐ Make party platters.
- ☐ Pick out an outfit and a pair of cool PJs.
- ☐ Create goodie bags.
- ☐ Run through the games and activities in your head.

## FIGURE OUT IF IT WILL WORK

Now that you've decided what kind of party you would like to have, you need to decide if it's doable. If you want a treasure hunt theme, decide if your home is large enough to accommodate your guests. If you had your sights on a round of basketball or Frisbee, is your backyard big enough? Do you have a playroom or den that you can use as your party room? Do you have your parents' permission to hang decorations, move furniture, and sleep in whichever room you decide is the party room? If it turns out that the party you had envisioned won't work, scale it down a bit. For instance, instead of decorating the whole house, you could decide to just concentrate on one room. Or instead of having the treasure hunt scattered around the house, limit it to just downstairs or just the living room.

"First, we ate pizza. Then we did karaoke. Everyone sang! Then Sierra made everyone laugh with her stories. I didn't know she was so funny. All that laughing made us hungry again. We baked yummy cookies, talked about crushes, and made friendship bracelets. I *never* felt homesick. I had the best time."

—*Yvonna, 11,*
*on her first sleepover*

### Share It with the Troops

Share your ideas with everyone on your guest list. Friends can add their own ideas, or help you tweak yours. Start a group chat with all your guests, or gather them around the lunch table one day. Throw your party theme out there to see what everyone thinks.

But remember—it's your party, and as long as you're prepared, organized, and courteous to guests, your party will be a success regardless of the theme you choose!

## SET THE PLAN IN MOTION

Start carrying out some of the tasks on your list. If you are crafty, make your own invitations and hand them out. You can use the invitations at the back of this book if you'd like, or create your own! (For invitation ideas that tie in well with different themes, turn to page 13.) Buy or make party favors, decide on decorations, and add a few special touches, such as colored lightbulbs that you can string across the ceiling in your party room, to make it feel magical. You can put as much or as little effort into each element as you'd like. Where you decide to focus your attention is up to you!

## BE PREPARED TO HOST

If you are the host, it's your job to take care of your guests. Be polite and friendly, and go out of your way to make sure that everyone has what they need. That could mean pouring drinks or arranging cheese and crackers on a platter while everyone else is relaxing on the couch.

Make everyone feel comfortable and special by spending a few minutes one-on-one with each guest. Show your thoughtfulness. If you know your friend Susie drinks soy milk, have some on hand when it's time for milk and cookies. If Jessie can't eat nuts, make sure you have snacks that are nut-free. You want your guests to have an awesome time—if they're having fun, chances are you will, too!

## HOUSE RULES

After you get the green light to host a sleepover party from your parents, prove to them that you are up to the challenge. Make sure you understand your parents' rules and expectations for the party. If their general rule is that you have to leave the room the way you found it before the party, let them know that you are willing to clean in preparation for the party, as well as clean up after the party is over. You could be extra efficient by asking a few friends if they wouldn't mind being on the clean-up crew with you.

# THE TOP 10 THINGS TO GET STRAIGHT

**Before the Party**

1. Look at the family calendar for a date that works for you and your parents.

2. Decide how many guests will be invited. If this is your first sleepover, go for a smaller group. A smaller group is easier to manage.

3. Set up a specific time for the party to begin and end, so that parents will know when to drop off and pick up their kids.

4. Decide on the menu. Will you serve snacks only? Or will you provide dinner and breakfast the next morning? After you decide, make a grocery list of all the food you need to buy.

5. Decide if the party will be gender-inclusive, meaning that both girls and boys will be invited. This is definitely something to discuss with parents beforehand. You'll also want to make sure that the other guests are comfortable with a co-ed slumber party.

6. Decide where the guests will sleep. Will it be in your room, or in another part of your home?

7. Do any of your guests have allergies or dietary restrictions? Make sure you make note of this when planning out your menu so you're only serving things everyone can eat!

8. Discuss which rooms of the house are off-limits to guests.

9. Agree, in advance, on a time when lights are out.

10. Establish a code with your parents to let them know you need a little help managing the party.

 *Share It with the Troops*

Once you have all these rules in place, text or e-mail them to everyone on the guest list. That way, there will be no surprises or misunderstandings, and everyone's parents will appreciate knowing the party rules.

## IT'S OKAY TO ASK FOR HELP!

Professional adult party planners know that they can't take care of all the party details alone. They enlist the talents of others to make the party come together. So it is up to you to assign some of the jobs or responsibilities to your friends. That is called *delegating*. Go ahead and put Marty and Sue on decorations, or Emma and Riley on compiling a movie and snack list. If you have an artsy friend, ask her if she can help make invitations. If you have a friend who's really into music, ask him to create a playlist. If you have a friend who loves to shop, ask her if she'd help you get some of the stuff you need.

Other partygoers may be willing to help:
- ❏ Clean up before the party.
- ❏ Clean up after the party.
- ❏ Prepare the refreshments.
- ❏ Set up the furniture in the party room.
- ❏ Give out game prizes.
- ❏ Decorate the room.

*Share It with the Troops*

Ask friends for their help. Match each friend to the task that they would be good at, like blowing up balloons or hanging decorations. Then tell them when you need their help. Would it be the night before the party, just before the party, or right after the party?

## SKIP THE STRESS

Try to keep the party plans moving along. Don't get too stuck on the details. You may have wanted to hang neon lights from the ceiling, but it ended up being too difficult. If you have a vision but things are not coming together the way you had hoped, that's okay! It happens to everyone. Things don't always go according to plan, but that shouldn't stop you or your guests from having a great time. A party, after all, is supposed to be fun, not stressful. If you start to feel stressed or anxious, you might consider simplifying the plan.

## WHAT MAKES A PERFECT FINISHING TOUCH?

Start thinking about simple touches that will create a party atmosphere, such as glow-in-the-dark necklaces, banners, balloons, flowers, candles, fabric throws, a pile of soft pillows, or colored lights. If your party has a theme, make sure that these decorations tie in with your theme. Show your plans to your guests and parents for their input.

## WHAT MAKES A COOL CENTERPIECE?

A centerpiece is a neat way to make a statement, and it can serve many purposes depending on the kind of party you're having. As the visual symbol of the party, it should interest your guests and capture the essence of the theme.

The centerpiece could be as simple as a basket filled with party favors, or a large framed photo of you and your friends. If you are thinking of doing a beach party theme, the centerpiece could be a sand pail with a colored beach ball right next to it and some sunglasses and seashells scattered around. Or you can decorate a plate with sea shells and pieces of sea glass.

If it's a birthday party, make the table bright and festive by throwing confetti and streamers all over the table. Then toss assorted wrapped candies all over your place settings.

To make a unique and easy floral arrangement, see "Flower Power Centerpiece" in Chapter 8: Time for Crafts (page 70).

## INVITATIONS

Keep your invitations simple and fun. What's most important when making invitations is to include all the party details: the date, address, time, RSVP, and if there's something you'd like your guests to bring (like sleeping bags and pillows!). Of course, you also want to include your own name on the invitation so your guests know who's inviting them.

There are many options for creating invitations. You can make them on your computer or by hand, or buy them from a store. You might want to design the invitation to look like a pillow or a pair of pajamas. On pages 19–27, more specific ideas for invitations are provided.

## Custom Notecards

A creative option you might consider is decorating plain notecards with markers, colored pencils, and an assortment of stickers or stamps. Add glitter, sequins, and other embellishments to give your invitations some extra personality. Once you're done decorating the notecards, punch a hole at the top and loop a small piece of ribbon through the hole. Tie the ribbon into a bow, et voilà! Your friends will be saying, "Are you *sure* you didn't buy these?!"

If you don't feel like getting crafty or if you'd rather spend more time on other party details, an e-vite might be the way to go. There are several websites where you can design your invitations digitally and send them out electronically, such as Evite, Paperless Post, and Punchbowl.

## Don't Forget to Include RSVP

RSVP essentially means "Let me know if you can come to my party so that I'll know how many party favors I'll need to get, how many hot dogs my dad will need to put on the grill, and how many place cards I'll need to write." When guests call to let you know if they can come, keep a guest list by the phone (or create a list in the Notes app on your phone) and check off each partygoer's name. Use this also as an opportunity to ask your guests if they own a sleeping bag, if they have any food allergies, and if they can help with the party in some way.

## RSVP, PLEASE!

**RSVP** stands for *"répondez, s'il vous plaît,"* which is French for "please reply." Nowadays, many invitations include a "regrets only" on the RSVP line. That means that as the host, you will count on seeing the guest at the party, unless she calls to tell you otherwise.

Why do we use the initials of a French phrase in invitations that are in English? Because the French have strong ideas about manners that come from the French court of King Louis XIV, from the late seventeenth and early eighteenth centuries.

## MENUS

You will want to serve food that all your guests can enjoy. That's not always easy, because lots of people have food allergies or dietary restrictions, such as being gluten-free or having a peanut allergy. You also may have guests who are vegan or vegetarian. Before planning the menu, ask your guests for their input. Find out what they can and cannot eat. You will want to plan food that is easy to prepare and fun to eat. (Check out Chapter 9 on page 81 for simple recipes.) You may have to offer a few choices to accommodate everyone. If cooking is not your thing, or if your parents don't want you guys in the kitchen for too long, invite each guest to bring a dish. That's called a potluck. But coordinate in advance so that you don't end up with five different versions of mac and cheese!

 *Share It with the Troops*

Share the menu that you are planning. Ask friends for feedback. If you are doing a potluck, you can set up a chat to find out what each person wants to bring.

## MUSIC

A party isn't really a party without music. Ask your guests to make playlists! If everyone makes one, you'll have plenty of great music to listen to throughout the night. You might ask some people to create dance mixes and others to find music that's more relaxing. You can also just play your favorite songs from a music-streaming site such as Spotify® or Pandora®. Sites like these have premade playlists, but some require a subscription, which costs money. Check with your parents first before setting up an account.

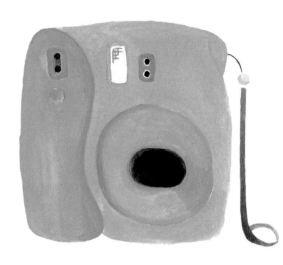

## CHERISH THE MEMORIES

Hang a large poster board in the party room. As guests arrive, ask them to sign and decorate the board. Have markers and pens ready. Hang the poster in your room as a memento of your amazing, ultimate slumber party!

Keep a camera on hand, or use the camera on your phone. During the party, you and your friends can capture all the fun by taking photos of one another. Polaroid® cameras are an especially fun item to have at a slumber party because the photos develop on the spot, right after they're taken! After you develop or download the photos, you can make a sleepover scrapbook.

### Share It with the Troops

There is always someone in the group who is a pro at taking photos. Ask them to take a pic of you and each guest. They can send the photos to everyone. That way, everyone can cherish the fond memories. Feel free to post these photos to social media, but make sure you have each guest's permission first. Some people might not want their pictures online, and that's something you have to respect.

# 2

# THEME PARTY

As discussed earlier, an awesome party often has an awesome theme. It's important to choose one that suits you and your guests. This section provides six classic party themes that will guarantee a night of fun. If none of these themes click with you, that's okay! You can use the ideas in this section as inspiration for a totally new and original theme. No theme is too wacky or weird—this is the time to let your imagination soar!

Let's say you want to have a party with an outer-space theme. Make the invitation resemble your favorite planet. Tell your guests to wear clothes with galactic elements. Serve dehydrated snacks and things astronauts would eat. See if anyone has a telescope you can use to look at constellations. Use glow-in-the-dark decorations. You get the idea!

## PARTY PROFILE QUIZ

Can't make up your mind about the perfect theme for your party? Take this party profile quiz to find a theme that perfectly suits you and your best friends. Circle the response that you most identify with.

**Your idea of total fun would be you and your friends . . .**
- A. playing basketball or hockey, throwing a Frisbee, or skateboarding.
- B. hiking, camping, and telling tales under the stars.
- C. reading and talking about your favorite books.
- D. listening to music, playing an instrument, and sharing opinions about your favorite music artists.
- E. going to the mall and window-shopping for the latest fashions.
- F. dancing, singing, and playing charades.

**You are best known for your love of . . .**
- A. sports.
- B. nature and animals.
- C. books.
- D. music.
- E. fashion.
- F. performing.

**Your style is . . .**
- A. athletic chic—basketball shorts, sneakers, ponytail.
- B. laid back—jeans, sweatshirt, comfy shoes.
- C. classic—khakis, sweater, barrettes, and headbands.
- D. rebel—faded jeans, boots, band T-shirt, leather jacket.
- E. runway-ready—designer dress, trendy accessories, high-heeled boots.
- F. theatric—Broadway T-shirts, colorful dresses, and fun makeup.

**It's important for you to . . .**

   **A.** get exercise.

   **B.** sit under the stars.

   **C.** talk about the last book you read.

   **D.** know whose album just dropped.

   **E.** wear your coolest accessories when leaving the house.

   **F.** show off your personality by telling stories.

**Tally Your Score!**

   ☆  If you answered most questions with **A**, host a Sports Night.

   ☆  If you answered most questions with **B**, choose the Under the Stars theme.

   ☆  If you answered most questions with **C**, have a Bookworm Bash.

   ☆  If you answered most questions with **D**, have a Music Party.

   ☆  If you answered most questions with **E**, host a Glam Girl Party.

   ☆  If you answered most questions with **F**, have a Stage Night Soiree.

# SPORTS NIGHT

Celebrate your active life and your love of sports with a high-energy party that's full of games and fun.

**Invitation Idea**

Make your invitation resemble a piece of sporting equipment, such as a tennis ball or a golf club.

**Wear**

Workout clothes, jerseys, or sweats.

**Eat**

Have foods that you might find at a sports event, like hot dogs, popcorn, and soft pretzels. Serve fresh fruit and energy bars.

**Activities**

OUTDOORS:

- ☆ Shoot hoops.
- ☆ Hold relay races.
- ☆ Ride bikes.
- ☆ Jump rope.
- ☆ Throw Frisbees.

INDOORS:

- ☆ Challenge one another in sports trivia.
- ☆ Read sports magazines.
- ☆ Watch sports events on TV.
- ☆ Discuss your favorite and least favorite sports players.
- ☆ Ask everyone which event they would want to participate in at the next Olympics.

**Favors**

- ☆ cool sneaker laces
- ☆ personalized water bottles
- ☆ energy bars
- ☆ sweat bands

# UNDER THE STARS

You are outdoorsy, so why not hold the party in your backyard under the stars? If possible, set up a tent so you and your friends can sleep outside. If the weather doesn't cooperate, bring the tent inside and set up camp in the living room. Put glow-in-the-dark stars on the ceiling and hang plants to create the feeling that you're surrounded by beautiful nature.

**Invitation Idea**

Draw a moon and stars on the invitations. Ask guests to bring flashlights.

**Wear**

Hiking and camping gear with neon-colored wristlets and colored bandanas.

**Eat**

Have a grill set up in the backyard for roasting vegetables and meat. Make and eat s'mores (check out the recipe in Chapter 9, page 87). Drink milk and eat freshly baked cookies in the shapes of moons and stars.

**Activities**

- ☆ Before it gets dark, go on a hike around the neighborhood. Make sure you bring enough water!
- ☆ When it's dark, play tag. Players can use their flashlights to shine some light on the game.
- ☆ See how long your guests can stay quiet to listen to the sounds of nature.
- ☆ Talk about what you hear.
- ☆ Have each guest wish upon a star.
- ☆ Share hiking adventures.
- ☆ Gather around a real or pretend campfire for a sing-along.
- ☆ Tell ghost stories.

**Favors**

- ☆ photos of the campers
- ☆ plastic canteens
- ☆ colored rocks and stones
- ☆ bags of homemade trail mix

# BOOKWORM BASH

You and your friends are bonded forever by your shared love of books—why not celebrate that with a book party? Talk about the stories that you have read, which characters you loved best, and which you loved least.

### Invitation Idea

Make the invitation look like a book. Draw a bookworm on the cover. Write the party info inside the folded invitation on the "open pages" of the book.

### Wear

Dress as your favorite book character and have your friends try to guess who you are. Stay in character for as long as you can.

### Eat

As you discuss character and plot, enjoy cups of hot chocolate or herbal tea. Crunch on chocolate-covered biscotti. Dine on foot-long "hero" sandwiches.

### Activities

- ☆ Play charades using favorite book titles.
- ☆ Write a group story. Pass around a notepad and have each person write a few sentences. Read the finished story aloud. Experiment with different genres like mystery, sci-fi, and romance.
- ☆ Create your own magazine. Each person could contribute an article!

### Favors

- ☆ books
- ☆ colored pencils
- ☆ journals
- ☆ bookmarks

# MUSIC PARTY

Throw a bash that focuses on your love of music. Dancing, singing, karaoke—your party can have it all!

### Invitation Idea

Make an invitation in the shape of large headphones or an oversize music note.

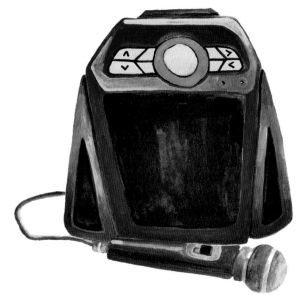

### Wear

Dress as your favorite musician, singer, or pop star. Can anyone guess who you are?

### Eat

Eat what musicians eat when they're on the road touring the country! Munch on raw foods, such as fresh fruits and veggies with hummus or spinach dip. Dine on vegetable and cheese sandwiches on French bread. Drink hot herbal teas or sparkling water to soothe your vocal cords.

### Activities

- ☆ Get in touch with guests before the party to find out their song requests. Then compile a playlist with everyone's choices. Have one of your friends act as the DJ to make sure that whatever song is playing matches the current mood of the party.
- ☆ Try karaoke.
- ☆ Mouth the lyrics of songs and have friends guess the titles.
- ☆ If you and your friends play instruments, have a jam session!
- ☆ Play musical chairs.
- ☆ Play air drums and air guitars, and when the music stops, freeze.

### Favors

- ☆ a CD with all your favorite songs or a shared playlist that all your friends have access to
- ☆ homemade drums and shakers made from coffee cans and dried beans

## GLAM GIRL PARTY

If you love getting dolled up and giving your friends makeovers, then this party is definitely for you! A glam girl party is filled with glitter, sequins, and everything fabulous. By the end of it, you and your friends will have transformed from slumber-party attendees into Hollywood VIPs!

*Share It with the Troops*

A glam girl theme gives you the perfect opportunity to host a fashion show. Make videos of each person's runway walk and share them with your friends via text or social media, as long as it's okay with everyone.

### Invitation Idea

In the invitation, tell your guests they've been invited to the most exclusive fashion event of the year!

### Wear

Glamorous outfits, complete with rhinestone-studded tops, faux-fur shawls, high heels, satin gloves, and lots of jewelry.

### Eat

Your favorite fancy foods, such as shrimp cocktail, mini meatballs, and grilled chicken skewers. For dessert, fill empty ice cream cones with fresh fruit salad.

## Activities

- ☆ Do beauty and hair makeovers.
- ☆ Give manicures and pedicures.
- ☆ Act like models and conduct a photo shoot.
- ☆ Have a fashion show. Give each guest a turn at walking down the runway. Take photos of each guest in a fabulous outfit.

## Favors

- ☆ photos of each girl on the runway
- ☆ bedazzled purses
- ☆ sparkling nail polish

### Share It with the Troops

Ask if anyone has any special makeup or hairstyling tips and is willing to demonstrate to the group! If not, google hairstyles and makeovers. Check out tutorials on YouTube™ to help you learn how to highlight and contour facial features, or how to curl or straighten your hair like the pros.

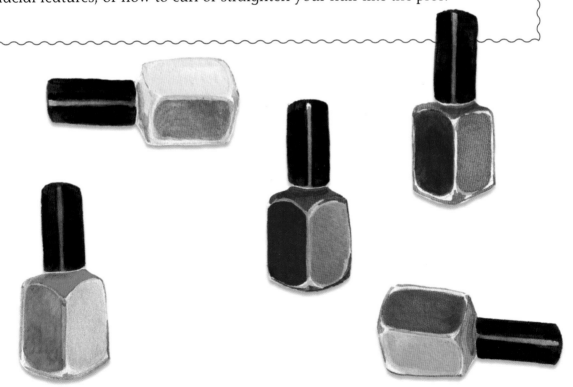

# STAGE NIGHT SOIREE

You and your friends love to perform, so turn your party into a stage event. Everyone's a star at this party!

### Invitation Idea

Make the invitation resemble a program for a play. Include your guests' names as a cast of characters or a list of activities you've planned labeled Act I or Scene 2, as in a real play.

### Wear

Dress like your favorite movie character or character from a play or musical.

### Eat

Go for the drama with colorful foods, such as tri-color pasta, or pizza piled high with salad. Or, ask guests to bring a favorite mystery dish, and have tasters guess what they are eating. And don't forget popcorn!

## Activities

☆ Fill a trunk with dress-up stuff: wigs, hats, gloves, boas, shawls, and sunglasses. Use these items as props for guests to try on to create new characters.

☆ Give each guest five minutes of fame. Let them act, sing, dance, do impressions, or tell jokes. Videotape it, if possible.

☆ Make up a dance routine and perform it for an audience.

☆ Talk about favorite movies.

☆ Create a routine to perform at the next local talent show.

## Favors

☆ sunglasses

☆ autograph books

☆ theater masks

# CHAPTER 3

# GREAT GUESTS

You've got what it takes to be a great host. But what happens when you're invited to a sleepover at someone else's house? Here are a few hints on how to be the best guest.

## WHAT TO PACK

Here's everything you'll need for your evening out:

- ❑ cell phone and charger
- ❑ special pillow (Better yet, make your own; see "Me Pillows" on page 72.)
- ❑ sleeping bag (or thick blanket)
- ❑ your favorite PJs
- ❑ fuzzy slippers
- ❑ hairbrush
- ❑ hair accessories
- ❑ toothbrush
- ❑ toothpaste
- ❑ hand towel
- ❑ jeans and a T-shirt for the next day
- ❑ camera (unless your camera is part of your phone)
- ❑ magazines
- ❑ small flashlight
- ❑ bathing suit (if the invitation suggests bringing one)

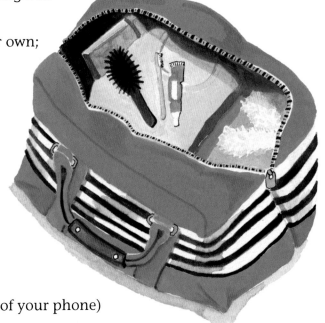

# HOW TO KEEP THE PARTY HOPPING

**Have a Positive Attitude**

Even if you're a little nervous about going to a slumber party, it's pretty likely that you're going to have fun in the end—just keep that in mind! Other guests may be feeling nervous, too, so try to give them a smile when you first arrive to ease both your nerves. Though it might not seem like much, a simple smile can go a long way.

**Be Up for Anything!**

Maybe you didn't plan on playing board games, or you thought that you would be having pizza for dinner instead of peanut butter and jelly sandwiches. Or, maybe you expected some other friends to be at the party. Well, whatever it is, don't get too bothered. Take a deep breath and let it go. Take the lead from your host, and try to have the best time possible. Keep an open mind and you might end up having more fun than you'd expected!

**Share Your Feelings**

What do you do if the conversation isn't flowing like a waterfall? Here are some ways to break the ice and keep the discussion lively:

☆ Talk about favorite songs, movies, books, and TV shows.

☆ Chat about funny things that have happened to you or members of your family. (Hint: Everyone loves a hilarious, embarrassing story!)

☆ What can you remember about a vacation? Did something unusual happen during a holiday break? Did you take a vacation to a special place?

After you tell your story, ask someone else to tell theirs, by asking something like, "Did something like that ever happen to you?" Give everyone a chance to speak. Don't worry about pauses in your chats. Conversation is an art that takes practice, and the more you practice the better you'll be at it. If all else fails, talk about your favorite celebrity crush. Everyone will most likely want to weigh in on that!

**Wear What's Comfortable**

If you are the host, let your guests know the dress code. Is the party casual or dressy? Do you want everyone to come in jeans or sweatpants, or be a little more dressed up? If you're a guest and the host hasn't told you they have a specific dress code, wear whatever you feel most comfortable in.

**Mind Your Manners**

Remember that you are a guest in someone's house, which means you should try your best to be polite to the host and their family. If their parents ask the group to quiet down, make an effort to be quieter. Make sure you pick up after yourself, and offer to help clean up. Basically, behave the way you would want the other guests to behave in your home if you were the host!

**Do . . .**
- ☆ clean up after yourself.
- ☆ offer to help with the dishes and clear away garbage.
- ☆ be friendly and polite toward your friend's family members.
- ☆ offer to help take photos, serve drinks, and set up games.

**Don't . . .**
- ☆ leave your belongings scattered about.
- ☆ open your friend's kitchen cabinets or the fridge without permission.
- ☆ wander around the house on your own.
- ☆ yell or make too much noise.

## "I WANT TO HAVE A SLEEPOVER, BUT . . ."

"I really want to have a sleepover, but the problem is Jimmy, my little brother. He is only four, but he is a huge pest. Jimmy acts up whenever I have friends over. He takes my stuff, makes embarrassing comments, and even hits me. I end up getting mad and yelling at him. How will I ever host a sleepover?"          —Bettina, 11

*Hey, Bettina,*

*Little brothers are sometimes hard to deal with, aren't they? Maybe your parents can talk to Jimmy. If he has a reward for good behavior set up with Mom or Dad, like a shiny new toy or a trip to the park, he might behave better. Or, maybe Jimmy can have a playdate planned for some of the time during your party. That will give you a nice breather. And when Jimmy does come home, you can let him meet your friends and share a snack before he goes to bed. That shouldn't be too painful!*

"I went to a sleepover a few weeks ago. Everything was going along fine, but then a couple of the girls started to argue about what games they wanted to play.

Things got out of control, and by the end of the party, three girls weren't talking to each other. I want to have my first sleepover, but I don't want anyone to fight."

—Mia, 10

*Hi, Mia,*

*Here are a few ideas to keep things cool at your first sleepover. First of all, think small. Don't invite more than three or four people. Also, have a plan. Know the games you'd like to play. Have several craft ideas and materials set up. Before the party begins, ask each guest to be up for some new things. Explain that the party will be more fun that way. Keep in mind that some girls might not want to play certain games. That's okay, too. Have a bunch of cool books and magazines on hand. They can hang out while the rest of you play.*

## "I WANT TO GO TO A SLEEPOVER, BUT . . ."

"I'm afraid that if I go to my friend's sleepover, I will get homesick. I don't know the girl too well, and I haven't met all her friends. She seems really nice, though. I want to go, but I don't know if I can handle it. What should I do?" —Marnee, 12

*Hello, Marnee,*

*How about going for at least part of the night? You can play games and get to know the girls, and if everything goes well, sleep over. Before the party, arrange to have a parent pick you up before lights-out, say at 10 p.m., just in case you have doubts toward the end of the evening. You can always change your mind. If anyone asks, just say that you're tired and you need the comfort of your own bed. But let the girls know how much fun you've had.*

"Okay, here's my problem. I snore really loud. I just moved here, and I don't feel comfortable enough to let these girls know. I don't want to be teased. I'm invited to a birthday sleepover for a girl named Monica. I want to go, but the snoring thing is telling me I should just stay home. What do you think?"

—Gracie, 12

*Howdy, Gracie,*

*A lot of people snore. It's not the worst thing in the world. Chances are, by the time everyone falls asleep, nobody will know you're a snorer because they will be out cold. Or, they might not hear you over their own snores. Remember this: we all make occasional embarrassing sounds. That's just the way life goes. Concentrate on making friends and just having fun.*

"I'm a health nut. I know I won't want to eat the food at the party. There's going to be pizza and cake, and I don't eat those things. I don't want to seem rude. Do you have any ideas for me?"
—*Talia, 13*

*Hello, Talia,*

*That's cool. Don't feel bad about being someone who eats healthful food. Here's what you do. Eat a good dinner at your house before you go. Bring a large platter of fresh veggies and hummus and ask the host if she wouldn't mind serving it so that you can have a snack. (Make it large enough, because I bet that some of the guests might want to have some, too.) You can also bring a bag of fruit, cheese, or nuts to leave in your friend's kitchen. When the girls eat a snack that you would rather not have, munch on one of your own snacks. If you don't make an issue out of it, nobody else will.*

# 4

# PARTY ICEBREAKERS

## GREAT GAMES TO GET YOUR PARTY STARTED

Your soccer pals don't know your school friends. Your school friends don't know your buds from acting class. And your buds from acting class don't even know you play soccer, let alone have friends from the team. How will you get all these good people together? Instead of putting your guests in a room to fend for themselves with small talk and bean dip, throw them into silly situations and let the games begin. Start the party with these games and challenges, and everyone will soon feel right at home.

**Write Positive!**

This easy icebreaker game makes everyone feel special! Write nice things about each other, and everyone will start warming up in no time.

BEFORE THE PARTY

Have colored construction paper, felt-tip pens, and tape on hand. Write each guest's name at the top of a piece of paper.

AT THE PARTY

Each girl gets a blank page taped to her back with her name written on the top. Then ask the girls to walk around the room and talk to each guest and write something positive about each girl they've met on the paper. For instance, Chloe's paper might say: very caring, animal lover, adventurous, loyal friend, kind, great laugh, pretty hair, cheerful. When everyone has finished writing compliments about each girl, remove the tape from the paper and let each guest read her positive comments. These make nice keepsakes and can be taken home and posted on a bedroom wall.

**Who Am I?**

It's a case of missing identity! As guests try to find out who they are, laughter fills the room.

BEFORE THE PARTY

Think of colorful characters from television, books, and movies. Write the names of these characters onto long strips of paper.

AT THE PARTY

Tape a strip of paper onto the backs of your guests as they arrive. Explain that everyone has to figure out who is posted on her back by asking the guests (who can read everyone else's back but their own) yes-or-no questions such as "Am I a female character?" or "Am I a superhero?" or "Do I do anything funny?" Guests should respond as if the person is really the character. When a guest correctly guesses her own identity, reward her with a small prize, such as candy or temporary tattoos.

### Play Forgetful

How observant are you? Do you notice when someone forgets something? Play this game to find out!

BEFORE THE PARTY

Ask each guest to come to the party with something out of place. Maybe they are only wearing one sock or they have lip gloss on only one side of the mouth. Maybe they're wearing two different shoes, two different earrings, or two different shoelaces, for example. (You may want to write this on the invitation.) Have paper and pencils on hand for your guests.

AT THE PARTY

Challenge your guests to put together a list of what each guest has out of place. The person with the most complete list wins the game—and is deemed the most observant!

### Don't Change the Subject

This game is hilarious because players must keep talking and talking and talking about one subject. Who will be the first to collapse into a fit of giggles?

BEFORE THE PARTY

Fill a party hat with crumpled-up colored strips of paper that contain words or phrases for players to use as conversation starters. Try some of these: Chinese food, amusement park, skeleton, string bean, potpourri, skateboard, blanket, or dinosaurs.

AT THE PARTY

Have one player at a time select a strip of paper from the hat, read it to herself, and immediately begin talking about the topic. The player must stay on the subject and keep making sense for three minutes, without stopping or pausing. Who will run out of things to say before changing the subject? Who will break down with a case of the giggles?

**Who Are You Talking About?**

How well do you know your guests? How well do your guests know each other? Play this game to break the ice and get everyone talking!

BEFORE THE PARTY

Write a fact about each guest. For example, you might write "born in another country," "has more than two brothers," "plays guitar," or "speaks Spanish." Write all of the statements together on one piece of paper, and give each guest a copy.

AT THE PARTY

As your guests mix, have them ask each other questions to determine whose name belongs with each statement. Whoever has the most names filled in after five minutes wins. The more people playing, the more fun this game is.

**Sign My Arm**

Now you don't need the cast to get the signatures! This game includes all the fun of signing casts without all the broken bones.

BEFORE THE PARTY

Have brown paper bags (lunch-size) for each guest. Also, have felt-tip pens for everyone.

AT THE PARTY

Have everyone place a paper bag over the hand and forearm with which she writes. This means if someone is right-handed, the bag will go over her right forearm. When you give the go-ahead, everyone in the room must get as many signatures as possible. Here's the catch: it's against the rules to sign with the hand that's covered. After three minutes whoever has signed the most bags wins the game. Try and find out whose names are on each player's paper-bag "cast." You might be surprised by how illegible some signatures are!

**Name That Guest!**

Do you have a nickname? Do you want one? Nicknames are fun, especially when good friends give them to you!

BEFORE THE PARTY

Have paper and pencils on hand. Also, have a hat.

AT THE PARTY

Divide the guests into pairs. Give each pair some time for chitchat. After a while, have the girls gather. Ask each girl to jot down a flattering nickname for the girl with whom she was paired, based on their chat. Have each girl write the nickname and place it into a hat without anyone seeing it. After all the nicknames are in the hat, say each one out loud and have the rest of the girls match the nickname with the right girl.

**Ask It Anything!**

While you're mixing and mingling, play a game that unlocks the mystery of your future.

Write a list of questions that require yes-or-no answers. Here are some suggestions:

☆ Am I going to get straight As?
☆ Will I be a cheerleader?
☆ Will I be a rocket scientist?
☆ Will I travel the world?
☆ Will I be rich?
☆ Will I get married?
☆ Will I have kids?

Copy the image shown on the next page onto a large poster board before the party. At the party, have a coin on hand.

TO PLAY

Give each girl a turn. Players ask the question aloud and then toss the coin over the game board. The coin lands on the response that answers your most pressing questions.

Count on it!

Try again. I'm not getting anything.

Probably not, but don't sweat it.

Better ask someone you trust for advice.

The answer lies in your heart.

There's a 50-50 chance that it will happen.

Not happening in this century.

Yes, most definitely!

# 5

# INDOOR GAMES

If you have bad weather on the night of your party, or it's gotten dark really early, or you'd just prefer to be indoors, these games will keep the fun going!

## PICKUP STICKS

This game is also known as jackstraws. You don't need much to play—just a pile of drinking straws.

**Before the party**

Have a pile of colored straws. (You can substitute with sticks or toothpicks.)

**At the party**

Hold a bundle of straws about six inches (fifteen centimeters) off the ground and then drop them. The first player tries to remove just one straw at a time from the pile without moving any of the surrounding straws. A player's turn ends when a straw wiggles as the result of taking away another straw. When the next player goes, they gather up the remaining straws and drop them again to create a new pattern of straws. The player with the most straws wins.

## GUESS WHO!

This game for four or more people is usually played outside, but it can also be fun in a large room without much furniture.

**Before the party**
You'll need a blindfold.

**At the party**
One player is blindfolded and stands in the center of the room. As the other players dart around her, she must try to tag them. When the blindfolded player tags another player, she then tries to guess who it is. For clues, she can try to touch the player's face and hair. When the blindfolded player correctly guesses the identity of the tagged player, that person puts on the blindfold and the game continues.

## EYES, NOSE, MOUTH

You have to be quick and focused with this game that tests your ability to follow directions.

**At the party**
Players form a straight line with a leader facing them. The leader says "Eyes, nose, mouth." When the leader says "eyes," the players touch their eyes. When she says "nose," players then touch the nose. But when she says "mouth," players must do what the leader does and not what she says. If the leader touches another body part, such as her left arm, when saying "mouth," the players should also touch their left arm. A player who touches their mouth, instead of doing what the leader demonstrates, is out of the game.

## SUSIE SAYS

Simon Says has been played since back in the days of Ancient Rome. Back then, Simon was Cicero, but the rule of being a sharp listener was still of the utmost importance. In our version, Susie is the leader—or you can change the name to whoever is the leader when you play!

**At the party**

The leader faces the players and makes simple commands such as "Susie says, place your hands on your hips," or "Susie says, shake your hands in the air." Players must follow the commands. But when the leader says, "Bring your hands down by your sides," the players must ignore the command because the leader did not say "Susie says" before the command.

## DO I KNOW YOU?

This is a good game to play if your guests are all friends. It tests just how well you know one another, and it can get pretty competitive!

**Before the party**

Have paper and pens on hand.

**At the party**

Pick someone to be the show's host, and divide the remaining guests into pairs. The host will ask everyone the questions from the list below. Each girl should write her answers on a separate sheet of paper and turn the paper over once she's finished writing. Peeking is against the rules! Once all the questions have been asked, then everyone can turn their papers over and see how many questions they've answered correctly. The premise of the game is that if you and your partner really know each other, you will get all the questions right. Pairs that answer the most questions correctly can celebrate by making friendship bracelets for each other.

- ☆ What color is your friend's room?
- ☆ Is she a dog lover or a cat lover?
- ☆ What does your friend want to be when she grows up?
- ☆ Does she prefer chocolate or vanilla?
- ☆ What's your friend's best sport?
- ☆ What toppings does your friend like on her pizza?
- ☆ What's her favorite book?
- ☆ What's your friend's favorite season?
- ☆ If your friend had a dream vacation, what would it be?
- ☆ What does your friend like on her hamburger?

- ☆ What was the biggest laugh you shared?
- ☆ Who's your friend's celebrity crush?
- ☆ If marooned on a desert island, what five things would your friend hope she had with her?
- ☆ Does your friend prefer pink, green, or black nail polish?
- ☆ What's your friend's favorite candy bar?
- ☆ What's her favorite song?

## WORK IT, GIRL!

How well do you work in a group? Can you cooperate with everyone like a well-oiled machine, or will your machine break down?

**Before the party**

Make a list of machines, such as a computer, popcorn maker, paper shredder, waffle iron, and elevator. Write each machine on a strip of paper, and throw the strips into a hat.

**At the party**

Divide the girls into teams of four. Explain that each team will pick a strip of paper out of a hat. The team will have sixty seconds to figure out a way to demonstrate what's written on the paper without using any props. Once each group has gotten its imaginary machine up and running, the other teams have to guess what kind of machine the team is using.

## HOLD IT

This game is similar to musical chairs. You have to act fast by listening to the music and keeping your eyes on the prize.

**Before the party**

Stuff a plastic bag with everyday objects, such as a roll of toilet paper, a shoe, a ruler, a book, a paper plate, a rubber glove, a box of crayons, a shoebox, and a tennis ball. Have as many objects as you'll have guests.

**At the party**

Start by placing all the objects on the floor. Play your favorite music while guests walk in a circle around the objects. When the music stops, everyone must grab an item. A person who doesn't grab an object in time is out. Take away one object before starting the music again, and put the remaining objects on the floor again. The winner is the person who manages to get hold of the last object.

## TONGUE TWIST

Challenge your friends to say a mouthful. Get ready to experience a laughing attack as everyone trips over their words.

**Before the party**

Write tongue twisters on strips of paper. Crumple them up and place them in a hat. Try some of the ones below or make up your own.

- ☆ Silly Sally should stop smirking.
- ☆ Big Billy bent Barbara's bear.
- ☆ Terry trusts Tia thoroughly.
- ☆ Lately, Lindsay looks luxurious.
- ☆ Julie just jumps for joy.

**At the party**

Have each girl take a turn trying a tongue twister. Players should say the phrase three times quickly without messing up.

## SHE DREW IT

How good are you at turning words into pictures? Can you communicate by drawing instead of speaking? It's much harder than it looks!

**Before the party**

Have pads and felt-tip pens ready for each player.

**At the party**

Explain to your friends that this is similar to the game telephone. Begin with a line of players, and give them all paper and felt-tip pens. The first player writes down a phrase, such as "Why did the chicken cross the road?" or "Girls rule, boys drool." Then the next player has to pass the message on as a drawing without talking or writing words. After she's completed her drawing, she folds the paper so only her drawing, not the original text, is visible. No peeking! The third person in line looks at the drawing and writes down her interpretation of it as a sentence, then folds the paper so only her sentence is visible before passing it on to the next player. Continue to alternate writing and drawing until everyone has seen the paper. Then compare the original phrase with the final drawing or phrase—the results are guaranteed to make you all laugh!

## CHOP-CHOP RELAYS

It's a race against time! You have to be fast, but you also have to be coordinated.

**Before the party**

You'll need two pairs of chopsticks, two brown paper lunch bags, two trays, and assorted buttons, hair combs, pencils, crayons, and spools of thread. Make sure you have as many items from each category as you have players.

**At the party**

Set up a course with a starting line and a finish line. In the middle area, arrange the buttons in one place, the hair combs in another, the crayons in another, and so forth. Divide the players into two teams. On the count of three, the first player from each team must pick up one of each object using the chopsticks and then drop it into the tray. The players must carry all the items to the finish line and drop them in the paper bag using chopsticks. Each team must collect items as quickly as possible—no time for slowpokes! The team who manages to get all their items in the paper bag first wins!

## UNDER YOUR SPELL

Ever notice how some words are unusually difficult to spell and even harder to pronounce? Test your grasp of the English language by having a spelling bee. Here are some really difficult words to try to spell with your friends. Remember, it's just for fun!

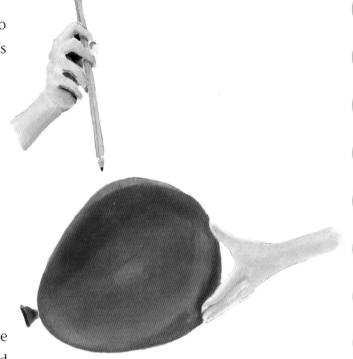

- ☆ plethora
- ☆ soothsayer
- ☆ conundrum
- ☆ pungent
- ☆ mediocre
- ☆ quell
- ☆ reincarnation
- ☆ cornucopia

## BALLOON BUST RELAY

Want a cool way to give out goodie bags? Put the loot inside balloons and use the filled balloons in a relay. Play this game outside, but in case of rain a large room that doesn't contain breakables will do.

**Before the party**

Buy large balloons. Stuff them with tiny prizes such as stickers, whistles, and temporary tattoos. Then inflate the balloons and tie them. You will need one balloon for each guest.

**At the party**

Divide the guests into two teams, and place each team behind a starting line. Place the balloons at the other end of the room. A player from each team must run to the other end of the room, grab a balloon, and pop it. She can pop it any way she wants as long as she doesn't use a sharp object. When the balloon pops, the player collects the prize and then races back to her teammates. The game continues until all balloons have been popped. The team that pops the most balloons wins.

## MUSICAL SLEEPING BAGS

This is a good game to play after everyone has changed into pajamas. It's like musical chairs, only harder!

**Before the party**

Arrange all the sleeping bags except one any way you want. Have a parent on hand to play music.

**At the party**

Have your friends parade around the room while the music plays. When it stops, each player must get in a sleeping bag in order to stay in the game. After each round, remove a sleeping bag. Keep playing until only one girl and one sleeping bag remain.

## HOLD HANDS

In this game, even easy tasks become a handful! Can you and your partner function with only one hand apiece? Or will working together turn into a clumsy mess?

**Before the party**

Have these materials on hand: a watch, a cord, a naked doll and doll clothes, a gift box, wrapping paper, tape, and a shoe.

**At the party**

Have players split up into pairs. Each pair stands hand-in-hand with their adjoining hands tied together with a cord. With their free hands (one with the right hand and the other with the left), the pairs must dress a doll, wrap a gift, and tie a shoelace. Which pair can complete these tasks in the least amount of time?

## PASS THE HAT

Could you pass a hat to a friend if you had to pass it without using your hands? It's not easy!

**Before the party**

Have two hats available. Use top hats or cowboy hats—anything with a strap won't work.

**At the party**

Have your friends form two circles, one inside the other. One player in each circle wears a hat. The object is to pass the hat around the circle. The only catch is, the players can't use their hands to pass the hat from head to head. They can use their feet, elbows, or necks. The team that passes the hat around the circle first wins.

## PASS THE PARCEL

In this unique way of gifting, everybody gets a prize. It's a win-win situation.

**Before the party**

Wrap a small prize, such as a keychain, lollipop, or candy necklace, in a layer of newspaper. Use a piece of tape to secure a different small prize to the top of the prize that was just wrapped. Then wrap another layer of newspaper around that and tape another prize on top. Keep doing this until you have wrapped at least one prize for each guest. Make sure the prize at the top layer is covered by newspaper.

**At the party**

Form a circle. Play music and pass the parcel around. Have someone volunteer to work the music. When the music stops, the player holding the parcel unwraps a layer of newspaper and gets the prize. Prize winners leave the circle so that each girl gets a present. You can also write fortunes, jokes, or messages on the newspaper to be shared with the crowd.

## GET DRESSED!

Does it take you a long time to get dressed in the morning? After playing this game, that should no longer be an issue!

**Before the party**

Fill two garbage bags with equal amounts of hats, scarves, mittens, shoes, belts, socks, and other accessories, plus oversize sweatshirts.

**At the party**

Two players compete against the clock to be the first one to put on all the items in the bag. Make it even more of a challenge by timing each player. Create teams and keep a tally of which team has the most wins.

## LIGHT AS A FEATHER, STIFF AS A BOARD

Spooky spirits might be present at your party, whether you invited them or not. Whose body will they lift?

### At the party

Dim all the lights and tell your guests to be very quiet. One girl lies on the floor. Everyone else sits around her on their knees with index and middle fingers resting under the girl's body. One person is the storyteller who sits by the head and tells a creepy tale about the life and tragic death of the person lying on the floor. At the end of the story, everyone chants "Light as a feather, stiff as a board," as they lift up the body a few inches (centimeters) off the ground with their hands. The idea is to have everyone believe that spirits are actually helping to lift the body off the ground. Take turns telling a story about each guest.

## CAN YOU DO IT?

Calling all trivia buffs! Be warned: If you can't answer these questions, you're going to face a silly task.

### Before the party

On small strips of paper, write your favorite trivia questions, such as "How many legs does a spider have?" or "Which planet is farthest from the sun?" Blow up balloons and insert a strip of paper with a question inside each balloon. Place these balloons in bag A. In bag B, have a bunch of blown-up balloons with silly commands written on strips of paper inside them. Here are some examples.

- ☆ Try to touch your nose with your tongue and lift your left leg in the air.
- ☆ Hold your arms up in the air for three minutes and recite a poem.
- ☆ Perform a dance routine and pretend you are a famous ballerina.

### At the party

When it's their turn, have each player reach into bag A, pull out a balloon, and pop it. If the player can answer the question correctly, she stays in the game for another round. If a player cannot answer correctly, she must pull a balloon from Bag B, pop it, and do what the paper inside says. If the player cannot carry out the command, she's out of the game. The game is over when all the questions have been answered. The person who answers the most questions correctly is the winner. Make a crown out of colored paper and write "Queen of Trivia" on it. The winner wears the crown for the night.

## MURDERER

Have you ever met someone with a chilling stare? What about a stare that could *kill*? In this spooky game, don't make eye contact or you might be the next victim!

**Before the party**

Get a hat and strips of paper. Have a strip of paper for each guest. Leave all the strips blank except for one. Write "murderer" on that strip.

**At the party**

Have each person pick a strip of paper out of the hat. On your mark, everyone will start walking around the room. The person who gets the strip that says "murderer" must select her victims while trying her best to remain undetected. She simply blinks at her victims to signal to them that they're being "murdered." When the victim realizes that she's just been murdered, she counts to three and falls to the ground—she can't talk anymore, and can't tell anyone who "killed" her! Then the players who are still alive have one chance to guess who's the murderer. If they guess correctly, they win! If they guess incorrectly, you keep playing until either the players guess correctly, or the murderer has "murdered" everyone. As everyone gets the hang of the game, your guests will become eager to stay alive! One important rule: players are not allowed to avoid eye contact.

## BE A STAR!

If you can sing, you'll enjoy this chance to perform. If you can't sing, you'll enjoy the chance to at least entertain.

**Before the party**

Set aside a place for three judges to sit. You may want to make paper hats or nameplates for them. Also, clear an area for the contestants to perform.

**At the party**

Your guests are invited to audition to become the next international singing sensation. Have each contestant belt out a tune. Be as serious or as silly as you want. Let the judges ask the contestants questions about the songs they picked. Then the judges must decide who is going to Hollywood and who is staying home. With permission, you can record these performances and post them on social media.

## PALM READING

If you spot a guest yawning or picking her teeth, it's time to show your friends your palm-reading talents. Your pals didn't know you could tell their fortunes, but now they will!

Palm reading, or palmistry, is the ancient art of reading the hands. A palmist may study the thumb, the lines on the palms, the shape of the fingernails, the fingerprint types, and all the markings in between the lines on the palm, to gain insight into a person's life and to see where her strengths and weaknesses lie. You may not be able to do all that, but you can read your friends' hands by following some basic palmistry principles.

**Basic palmistry principles**

Read the active hand. If someone is right-handed, read the right hand. If someone is left-handed, read the left hand. (The passive hand is used to read inherited characteristics.)

There are three main lines on the palm. The top line is the heart line, the middle line is the head line, and the bottom line is the life line. (Learn these lines by heart.)

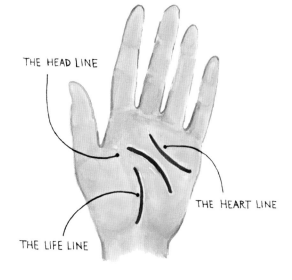

THE HEAD LINE

THE HEART LINE

THE LIFE LINE

Every hand is unique. No two are exactly alike. But the lines on your hands change. They stretch, disappear, widen, lengthen, and shift with time.

Now you can look at the three main lines on each guest's palm, and interpret what they might mean. Share what you find with them. Then your friends can compare their palm lines. What do they see about themselves? About each other?

## Matters of the heart

The heart line is the top line. It is closest to the fingers.

If your heart line is high and far from the middle line, you have great passion. But you may also be a little on the jealous side. A lower heart line—that is, a line closer to the middle line—means you are a balanced person. A heart line that curves upward is a sign that you are outgoing and emotional. If your heart line is curved as it runs across your hand, you are romantic and poetic. The more sweeping and curved a heart line is, the more romantic and passionate you are. If your heart line is not one clear line, but resembles a line of chains, you are a big flirt.

## Using your head

The head line is the middle line. It tells about your personality.

The stronger the head line is, the more forceful your personality tends to be. If the head line runs straight across, you are a focused person. A short head line that is strong means you can concentrate fairly deeply. You may be really good at projects that take a lot of patience, such as crafting and making jewelry. If you are imaginative, you will probably have a well-formed and slightly sloping head line.

## Life on the line

The bottom line (more vertical and curved), known as the life line, refers to how a person lives their life, not how long a person will live.

A longer line means that you get out there and live—you take advantage of all your opportunities. If your life line is a good distance from your thumb, you are generous with your time and energy.

## HEAD-2-PILLOW

Nobody will be bored with this board game. Share your personality and your opinions with the room as you move across the board.

### Before the party

Create a board or path like the one shown below. Make playing pieces with each girl's name written on a piece of cardboard or construction paper cut into a cool shape. Flip a coin to move about the board. Heads means move one space. Tails means moves two spaces. Or toss a single die.

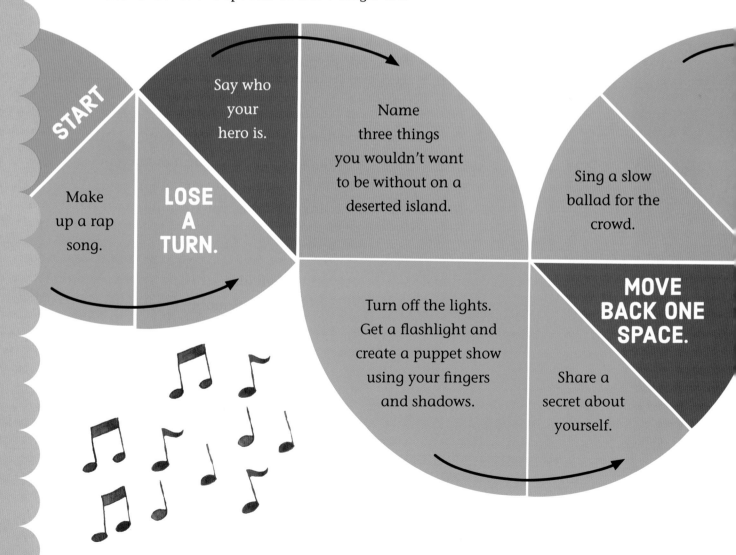

MOVE BACK ONE SPACE.

Tell your pals a bedtime story.

FINISH

MOVE BACK TO START.

Which TV character do you most resemble?

If your pillow could talk, what would it say?

Describe an awesome day in your future.

If you could invent something, what would it be?

Create a cool handshake for you and your friends.

LOSE A TURN.

SKIP AHEAD A SPACE.

Explain the plot of your favorite book.

Sing the jingle from your favorite TV commercial.

MOVE AHEAD TWO SPACES.

Describe your dream outfit.

# 6

# OUTDOOR GAMES

Being outside can add a whole new level of fun to your party, but there are a lot of safety factors to keep in mind. If it's hot outside, be sure to use bug spray and sunscreen. If you know you have outdoor activities planned, clear the play area before guests arrive so that it's free of sharp objects such as broken glass or nails. If you or your parents don't feel comfortable with guests running around barefoot, make a rule that everyone has to wear shoes outside. Your parents know your backyard the best, so ask them if there are any other safety hazards that you should be aware of.

Some of these outdoor games involve getting wet. If that's the case, make sure you tell guests in advance to bring their bathing suits.

## HUNT IN THE DARK

What objects can you find in the dark? Turn your flashlight on and call a search party.

### Before the party

Hide some cool stuff out in the backyard, such as small rubber spiders, headbands, bracelets, key chains, temporary tattoos, whistles, barrettes, wrapped candy, and nail polish. You'll need a flashlight for each girl.

**At the party**

Give each girl a flashlight, a small bag to collect items, and a list of things to find. Let the search begin. Who can find the most objects? In this game, the saying "finders keepers" definitely applies!

## NARROW NECKS

This is the perfect game to play when it's warm out. Players will need lots of space to run and it's likely that water will be spilled. Hope you're okay with getting drenched!

**Before the party**

You will need two beach chairs, an area in which to run, two large plastic pitchers, two blindfolds, access to a hose, and two empty 2-liter soda bottles.

**At the party**

Divide your pals into two teams. A person from each team sits on a beach chair, holding the empty bottle between her knees as still as possible. A player from each team is handed a pitcher filled with water. Both players get blindfolded and race to the seated player. Then the blindfolded player must pour the water from her pitcher into the bottle. The team that fills up the bottle first wins.

If you don't have pitchers handy, you can just use large plastic cups.

## SPIDER

Latch on to your friends to form a giant spider. Then make your way to the finish line. Whatever you do, don't let go! This is a good game to play on the sidewalk or in your driveway.

**Before the party**

Have colored chalk or tape and a whistle.

**At the party**

Make two circles, a starting line, and a finishing line with the chalk or the tape. Divide the players into two teams. Have each team huddle together inside the circles that were drawn. Make sure everyone is behind the starting line. Then have everyone in each team link arms around each other to create two giant spiders. When the whistle blows, both "spiders" must make their way to the finish line. Try to stay linked. If you come apart, you will have go back to the starting line. Which spider will win?

# WATER BALLOON VOLLEYBALL

Prepare to get wet. Very, very wet! Experience playing volleyball not needed.

### Before the party

Set up lots of water balloons and store them in a bucket. You'll need a volleyball net that cuts across the yard and at least one beach towel for every two players.

### At the party

Divide the guests into two groups that stand on opposite sides of the net. Divide everyone into pairs and give each pair a beach towel. Whichever side decides to start, that pair must place a water balloon in the center of their towel, and then lift the water balloon up by the towel's corners. The objective is to then toss the water balloon over the net using the towel and have the opposing side catch the balloon in their towel. The volley continues until one side fails to catch the balloon and the balloon bursts, giving the other team a point. If you don't have a net, have two pairs volley back and forth from towel to towel. Or, you could try tossing the water balloon without a towel.

## WATER LIMBO

It's time to limbo. How low can you go? And while you're at it, can you stay dry?

**Before the party**
Set up the hose.

**At the party**
Make sure your guests are prepared to get wet. Have one person hold the hose, and have everyone else limbo under the stream of water. Every time someone goes under it, lower the hose an inch. If someone touches the stream of water, they're out. Whoever is driest at the end of the game is the winner.

## WATCH OUT FOR THE SNAKE

Did someone say *snake*?! You can try to make a run for it, but the snake still might get you!

**Before the party**
Set up the hose and have a blindfold on hand. Also, set up parameters in the yard for where the playing field should be.

**At the party**
Have everyone pretend that the hose is a snake. Blindfold one person who holds the hose and moves the stream of water around. Everyone's objective is to try and dodge the water. Once you get hit by the water, you're out of the game. The last person standing is the winner.

## GO THROUGH HOOPS

Watch out! Obstacles are everywhere! Get ready to run, jump, toss, and hula hoop your way through the course.

**Before the party**

Arrange a course for your guests by setting a trail of outdoor obstacles—run around cones, climb over walls, crawl under cargo nets, jump through hoops, etc. Add other challenges, such as a beanbag toss, a jump rope, and a hula hoop. Make up rules for how to overcome each challenge, for instance: "You must jump the rope ten times," or "The hula hoop has to go around your waist five times."

**At the party**

Challenge your guests to go through the course as fast as they can! Award the one who makes it through the course in the best time with a prize.

# THE HOME SPA

Everyone loves to be pampered. Creating a spa experience right at home can make for an awesome sleepover. It makes everyone feel refreshed and relaxed. Here's how it works.

Set the tone by playing classical or New Age music. Serve some calming herbal tea and set out a veggie platter so your guests have something to munch on while sampling various beauty treatments. Of course, we know that your hair, nails, and skin look beautiful just the way they are; this home spa is just for fun.

You'll need a large room with enough chairs for each girl. Also, you'll need access to a sink, and a work space for mixing and mashing ingredients. If you're doing manicures and pedicures, you'll need a work space for that, too. You might ask your parents if you can use their master bathroom.

The best way to set up your spa is to create three separate stations: one for the hands and feet, another for the face, and a third for hair.

## TEN STEPS TO A GREAT SPA PARTY

1. Take photos of yourself and your guests before their beauty treatments begin. You'll find these photos useful later when you compare them with your after photos!

2. On the invitations, make it clear what the guests need to bring. Maybe they need to bring their own plastic tubs for soaking feet as well as their own towels, and you will supply everything else.

3. Try to enlist helpers beforehand, such as your parents, siblings, or friends, to gather supplies and mix the beauty treatments. Or you can make the mixing one of the activities at the party!

4. Don't rush through each spa treatment. Relax—you have all night.

5. Be practical. You can't completely transform your party room into a spa, but adding a few details will make all the difference in atmosphere. For example, hang a banner with the name of your spa on it (the name can be *anything*—get creative!), light some scented candles (get your parents' permission first), and put out piles of magazines.

6. Give everyone a chance to be pampered. Also, give everyone a chance to be a helper.

7. Make sure you protect all work surfaces and have supervision when it comes to mixing the ingredients.

8. Make sure everything is clean before going to bed. You can use the time when other girls are being pampered to pick up small messes here and there. This way, you won't have a huge mess to clean up later. Keep paper towels handy in case of spills.

9. Flip-flops make a perfect party favor for a spa party. Friends can wear them as their toes are drying after pedicures.

10. Take after shots once the spa experience is over. Put the before and after photos into a scrapbook, or add them to the goodie bags for guests to take home.

## HANDS AND FEET STATION

**Hands On!**

Here's a simple way to give a manicure:

1. Before taking out the nail polish, make sure you cover the surface with paper towels or old newspapers to avoid getting polish on furniture. Also, make sure

the room is well-ventilated. Crack a few windows open so that the fumes from the nail polish (which can be dangerous if you breathe in too much) have somewhere to go.

2. Soak hands, one at a time, in a small bowl with warm water and scented soap.

3. Dry each hand. Remove any old nail polish with a cotton ball and nail polish remover.

4. Trim nails with a nail clipper.

5. File nails with an emery board or a regular nail file.

6. For a special treat, massage each hand with scented cream. Rub the palm area and lightly tug on each finger.

7. Ask what color(s) your friend wants her nails to be painted. Apply clear or colored nail polish and a protective top coat.

8. Let dry.

9. If you wish, apply decals.

## CAUTION

We all know that sharing hair brushes can increase the spread of head lice. If you feel uncomfortable with the idea of sharing brushes and combs with guests, you can request on the invite that guests bring their own. You can also pass an infection or even nail fungus to someone else or even from nail to nail by sharing nail clippers. You may want to have your friends bring their own nail tools, or consider giving small nail kits out as goodie bags. Of course, it is perfectly all right to share prepared face masks and other pampering lotions and potions.

Do *not* ever use a hair dryer near water, or you can be electrocuted. Make sure your hands are dry whenever you are touching a hair dryer.

**Feet Up!**

Every foot loves a pedicure. Before the polishing stage, put your friend's feet in a foot bowl to soak in a sweet-smelling concoction (see recipes below!). Then use a foot brush or pumice stone to rub off the flaky skin. The next step is to apply moisturizing lotion and massage it into the feet and calves. This will feel very relaxing! And last of all comes the nail polish to ensure that all ten toes look adorable!

Here are two sweet potions to make tired feet feel like new again.

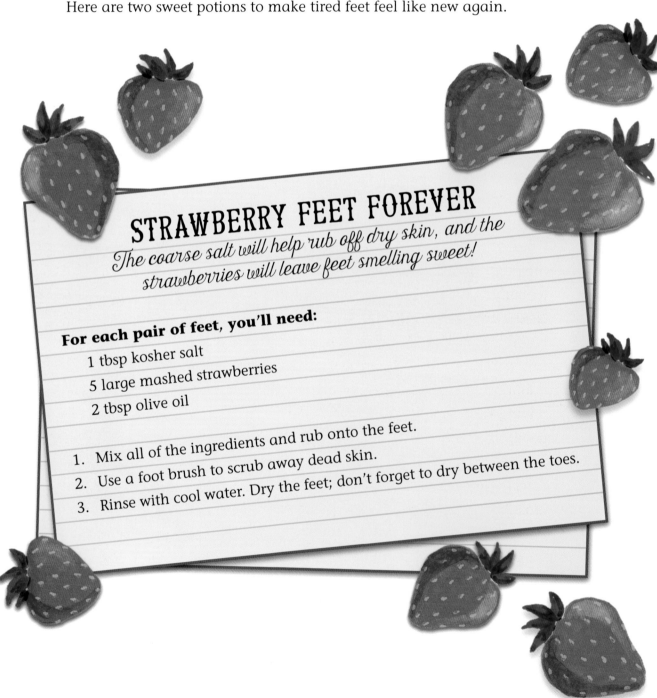

## STRAWBERRY FEET FOREVER

*The coarse salt will help rub off dry skin, and the strawberries will leave feet smelling sweet!*

**For each pair of feet, you'll need:**

1 tbsp kosher salt
5 large mashed strawberries
2 tbsp olive oil

1. Mix all of the ingredients and rub onto the feet.
2. Use a foot brush to scrub away dead skin.
3. Rinse with cool water. Dry the feet; don't forget to dry between the toes.

# HAPPY FEET!

*The lemon and cinnamon will smell heavenly, and the milk and oil will moisturize the skin and leave it feeling supple.*

**For each pair of feet, you'll need:**

1 cup lemon juice

5 shakes of cinnamon

2 tbsp olive oil

4 cups milk

1. Mix all of the ingredients and pour into the foot bowl.
2. Soak feet for 10 minutes.
3. Rinse with cool water. Dry the feet; don't forget to dry between the toes.

PEDI TIME!

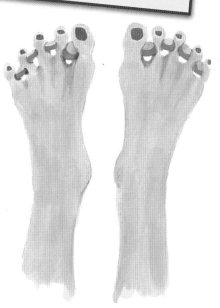

1. Once feet are clean and soft, it's time to clip the nails with a nail clipper. Beware of cutting toenails too short.

2. Next, smooth a nail file across each nail to buff and polish.

3. When nails are smooth and even, it's time for a foot rub. There are many health benefits to having your feet rubbed. Not only does it feel good, but it also relaxes the muscles in your feet, and it can lower your blood pressure. After adding a little bit of lotion to your hands, massage each foot gently with your fingers by kneading the skin in different directions. Most people love the way a foot massage feels. It revives tired feet and makes you feel totally relaxed from your head to your tootsies.

4. Next, apply a coat of polish to the nails. Add a clear top coat for sheen. Let toes dry for at least twenty minutes. If you have a small fan or two, you can place them near the feet to help dry the polish.

## FACE STATION

Here are seven steps to prepare the face for the fun:

1. Wash it.
2. Pat it.
3. Mask it.
4. Rinse it.
5. Tone it.
6. Refresh it.
7. Moisturize it.

Remember to ask your friends to bring their own face and hand towels. You might want to have a pile of clean washcloths on hand, just in case. You don't want guests spreading germs by sharing towels. As each person is done, throw their towel in a plastic bag to take home to be washed. If the towels are yours, throw the used ones in a laundry basket.

Be sure to keep all face masks, toners, and lotions away from the eyes and mouth. Some skincare products can burn or harm your skin if they are not used correctly. Make sure you read the directions on the label before applying. If someone has a reaction to a product, or if the product gets into someone's eyes, have the person flush out the area with water. Ask a parent for assistance.

## Exfoliate

Exfoliators help remove dry or dead skin cells. Along with other ingredients, they can be made with (dry) rolled oats and kosher salt. If you want to gently scrape away dead skin, try this mask.

### OATS 'N' HONEY MASK

**Per face:**

2 tbsp rolled oats

2 tbsp plain yogurt

2 tsp honey

1. Mix up the ingredients in a bowl, and apply the mixture to your or your friend's face.
2. Rub lightly with fingertips in circular motions.
3. Rinse with warm water, and pat dry.

## Tone

Astringents, which are water-based products meant to remove excess oil and tighten pores, help tone the skin. They create a more balanced face color throughout. Along with other ingredients, they can be made with lemon juice or grapefruit juice. To get that just-right skin, try the two astringents below.

### LEMON-UP MASK

**Per face:**

1 egg white

juice of 2 lemons

1. Whisk the egg and the lemon juice together in a small bowl, and apply the mixture to the face.
2. Leave on for 10 minutes.
3. Rinse with warm water, and pat dry.

# GRAPEFRUIT DELIGHT

**Per face:**

1 egg white

2 tbsp grapefruit juice

1. Mix up the ingredients, and apply the mixture to the face.
2. Leave on for 10 minutes.
3. Rinse with warm water, and pat dry. The skin will glow!

**Soothe**

Soothers refresh and revitalize tired skin. Try this remedy of sliced cucumbers to relieve puffiness under the eyes.

# CUCUMBER COMFORT

**Per face:**

2 slices of cold cucumber

1. Cover each eye with a slice.
2. Lean back and relax. Think about relaxing on a tropical island.
3. After about 3 minutes, discard your used cucumber slices.

## Steam

A steam treatment relaxes and soothes your face, but be careful not to burn yourself. Have an adult supervise this one!

### STEAM TEA TENT

**Per face:**

2 cups water
2 to 3 herbal tea bags (Chamomile is good)
hand towel

1. Bring the water to a boil. Carefully pour the water into a large heat-resistant bowl.
2. Add tea bags and let cool for a few minutes so that it's not scalding hot.
3. Cover your head with the hand towel and put your face over the bowl. There should be at least 6 inches between the bowl and your face. Breathe in the steam from the bowl.

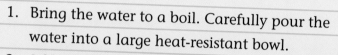
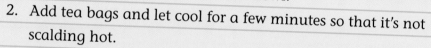

4. Enjoy for about 5 minutes until your skin feels dewy.
5. Rinse your face and pat dry.

## Moisturize

Moisturizers make skin smooth, supple, and silky. Mineral oil, beeswax, cocoa butter, avocado, and banana are all natural moisturizers that replenish the oils in the skin. Try the Happy Banana mask or the Milk 'N' Honey mask on the following page to get healthy, glowing skin.

# HAPPY BANANA

**Per face:**

2 bananas

1 tbsp honey

2 tbsp sour cream

1. In a small bowl, mash up the bananas with a fork, then whisk in the honey.
2. Coat the face with the mixture. Keep it on for 15 minutes.
3. Gently wipe it off with a wet washcloth, making sure to rinse any excess off of your face. Pat dry.

# MILK 'N' HONEY MASK

**Per face:**

1 egg white

1 tbsp honey

3 tbsp powdered milk

1 tsp liquid glycerin (from a drugstore)

1. Mix all of the ingredients in a small bowl.
2. Apply to the face with a brush or fingers. Use all of the mixture.
3. Relax for 15 minutes.
4. Rinse with warm water, and pat dry.

## LOTIONS AND POTIONS

It's always a good idea to have a variety of store-bought face creams and lotions on hand. Let the guests try on their favorites. You may want to ask your friends to bring moisturizers from home to share.

## HAIR STATION

Before you start styling, condition the hair with one of these two mixtures. Conditioning the hair helps nourish it, especially if it's dry or brittle.

### MAYO HALO

Take **2 cups of mayonnaise** and **1 tablespoon of lemon juice**, mix, and massage it into the scalp. Wrap hair in plastic for 10 minutes. Rinse well. Run **a few tablespoons of lemon juice** through the hair as you are rinsing to make the hair smell good. This is ideal for normal hair (hair that is neither too oily nor too dry).

### HONEY BANANA

Mash **one ripe banana** in a small bowl. Add **1 teaspoon honey**. Massage into wet hair and leave in for 10 minutes. Rinse well with warm water or seltzer for added shine.

# TIME FOR CRAFTS

**F**eel like getting crafty? Try some of these projects. Most are easy, but check the Project Difficulty Meter before tackling them. You may want to ask your guests to bring supplies or materials with them to the party. Otherwise, the crafts can get expensive. You can include what guests need to bring on the invitation so that they will have time to prepare.

## WHERE TO FIND SUPPLIES

When was the last time you checked out your local craft store? If it has been a while, or if you've never been inside a craft store, it might be worth a visit! Ask your parents to take you, and bring a few friends along to make a fun trip out of it. If you don't have any craft ideas beforehand—don't stress! You'll get lots of inspiration just walking up and down the aisles. You'll find neat kits for home-made key chains, T-shirts, jewelry boxes, stuffed animals, masks, and much more. You'll also find the materials you need to accessorize hats or personalize shopping bags Whatever project you decide to do, the crafts store will help make your slumber party a major success!

## PROJECT DIFFICULTY METER

Are you looking for an easy project to keep you and your friends busy for about fifteen minutes, or are you thinking of something a little more involved? Check the Difficulty Meter rating before undertaking any project.

- ☆ **1** = It's easy and fun (approximate time: fifteen minutes).
- ☆ **2** = This memorable keepsake will require a little preparation time, patience, and commitment (approximate time: thirty minutes).
- ☆ **3** = You'll need to concentrate and use your imagination in order to create this special item (approximate time: one hour).

Projects that involve glue may take a little extra time to dry. See individual project directions.

# ME PILLOWS
## PROJECT DIFFICULTY METER = 3

You can make these Me Pillows as gifts for your guests before the party, or even better: you can create them together! On the invitations, ask your guests to bring their own old or inexpensive pillow cases, or pillows that they would be willing to use in a craft project. You might also consider asking them to bring their own fabric scraps. The coolest pillows are the ones with personality, so encourage your guests to get creative.

**You'll Need:**

- newspaper
- pillow cases or pillows (Find pillow cases and pillows in a craft store, or reuse old throw pillows.)
- fabric scraps, ribbons, and bows
- scissors
- buttons, beads, or sequins (optional)
- fringe, faux fur, yarn, and decorative borders
- fabric glue
- permanent marker
- scented spray, like lavender or fruit
- pillow stuffing

1. Before you begin, cover the work surface with newspaper. This will make the clean-up process much easier.
2. Decorate your pillow or pillow case with a variety of materials. Use colorful fabrics to make your own facial features. You can use buttons to make your eyes, felt scraps to make your nose and lips, and yarn to make your hair. Glue these to the pillow's surface. You can always embellish further with buttons, beads, or sequins. Just keep in mind that if you plan on resting your head on the pillow, you'll want to keep the surface somewhat smooth.
3. Write your name on the pillow using permanent marker, along with some words that describe you. Add a fringe or a neat border to create a frame around your self-portrait.
4. Spray the finished pillows with scented spray, if you wish.

**NOTE:** If you are using a pillow case to make a pillow, fill it with stuffing. Seal the open end with fabric glue. Let it dry for about an hour. Follow steps 2–4 to complete the project.

# FLOWER POWER CENTERPIECE
### PROJECT DIFFICULTY METER = 1

Make this as a centerpiece for your party, or ask your guests to bring an empty coffee can and a package of colored straws so they have a centerpiece to take home and put in their room. You can provide the rubber bands, ribbons, and flowers.

**You'll Need:**

    1 large empty coffee can per guest
    1 package of colored plastic straws for each coffee can
    2 wide, long rubber bands per can
    wide spool of ribbon
    fresh, dried, or plastic flowers

1. Wrap 2 rubber bands around the center of the coffee can. Line the outside of the can with a columns of straws, and secure them by placing them under the rubber bands. If done correctly, no part of the coffee can should be showing.
2. Hide the rubber bands by tying a pretty ribbon around them.
3. Fill the vase with your favorite plastic or real flowers.

# HANGING PICTURE FRAMES
## PROJECT DIFFICULTY METER = 2

Decorate the party room with these hanging framed photographs! On your invitations, tell guests to bring photos of themselves.

**You'll Need:**

- photos
- wrapping paper
- craft sticks (or Popsicle sticks), 4 for each guest
- felt-tip pens or markers
- fabric glue
- colorful yarn
- scissors

1. Cover the work surface with newspaper.
2. Cut strips of festive wrapping paper. Make sure they are large enough to completely cover one craft stick.
3. Coat each of the four craft sticks in glue and cover with wrapping paper.
4. Tie a long piece of colored yarn around one craft stick. Attach the yarn to middle of the stick so that the frame will hang as a square.
5. Attach your photo to the frame by putting glue on the borders and pressing the two together. Keep applying pressure until you think the glue has dried.
6. Tie the yarn to a doorknob, or tack it to the ceiling.

# SILLY SLEEPING MASKS
## PROJECT DIFFICULTY METER = 2

Make masks that capture your personality and block out the light while you're asleep. These masks might come in handy the day after the party—when you're in need of a serious nap! Encourage your party guests to wear their fancy sleep masks to bed.

**You'll Need:**

cardboard cutout of an eye mask
(You can make this by tracing
a real eye mask.)
scissors
various kinds of felt and googly
eyes

felt-tip pens or markers
colorful yarn
hole punch
fabric glue
elastic strip

1. Cover the work surface with newspaper.
2. Let each guest use the cardboard cutout to trace the shape of the eye masks onto felt or fabric.
3. Cut the masks out with scissors.
4. Have the girls decorate their eye masks with relaxing bedtime sayings, such as "Sleep Tight" or "Sweet Dreams." Guests can draw thick eyelashes onto the masks, or they can decorate them with googly eyes or drawn-on Zs.
5. Create holes on both sides of the mask using a hole punch. Secure a piece of elastic through the hole on one side of the mask, and holding the mask up to cover your eyes, measure the elastic strip across the back of your head. Make sure the elastic is not too tight. Secure the elastic to the other side by tying it through the opposite hole.

**NOTE:** Don't use glitter or anything that might easily get into the sleeper's eyes.

# FLOWER CROWNS
## (AND OTHER HAIR ACCESSORIES)
### PROJECT DIFFICULTY METER = 1

Flower crowns are the perfect accessory for concerts and festivals—and they're fun to make, too! Embellish yours so that the next time you attend a public event, you'll stand out from the crowd.

**You'll Need:**

> metal barrettes
>
> black elastic ponytail holders
>
> fabric headbands (usually available at craft or fabric stores)
>
> embellishments, such as fake flowers, ribbons, fur trim, sequins,
>     beads, and whatever else you can think of!
>
> various fabrics
>
> fabric glue

1.  Cover the work surface with newspaper.
2.  Glue the chosen flowers, fabric, sequins, or beads to the headbands, barrettes, or ponytail holders. Let them dry for about an hour. You can also simply tie a piece of fur trim or a colored bow to an elastic ponytail holder.
3.  Give each guest a small plastic bag or a pretty gift box to hold her beautiful new hair accessories.

**NOTE:** While you're waiting for your hair pieces to dry, play Ask It Anything from Chapter 4 (page 37).

# COOL CAPS

**PROJECT DIFFICULTY METER = 2**

Create a unique sporty look by decorating a baseball cap! On the invitations, you can ask your friends to bring a plain baseball cap to decorate. If you and your guests are splitting up into teams for the games in Chapters 4 through 6, you can use these hats as swag for the team and decorate them according to the team name and team colors. If you don't plan on playing any team games, you can decorate according to your individual style!

**You'll Need:**

baseball cap for each guest
fabric paint
fabric glue
an assortment of beads, sequins, and rhinestones

1. Cover the work surface with newspaper.
2. First, decide on a name for each team. Then select team colors and design a team logo with your teammates. If you're not using these hats for team games, skip this step.
3. If you're using these hats as team swag, write the team name and logo onto the hats using fabric paint. If you're not using these hats for team games, skip this step.
4. Adorn the hats with beads, sequins, and rhinestones using glue. Allow about an hour for the glue to dry.

# TREASURE BOXES

## PROJECT DIFFICULTY METER = 2

Make beautiful boxes to keep your most precious items safe. On the invitation, you can ask guests to bring an empty shoe box or wooden box and a few old magazines.

**You'll Need:**

- glossy magazines
- strips of colored tissue paper
- scissors
- empty shoe box or wooden box
- regular glue or wood glue
- glitter

1. Cover the work surface with newspaper.
2. With scissors, cut out pictures from your favorite magazines.
3. Glue strips of tissue paper and the magazine cutouts onto the box. Let dry.
4. Brush on a top layer of lacquer glue over your paper decorations. For a sparkling effect, add glitter to the box when the glue is still wet. Let the box dry overnight.

# SWEET SACHETS
## PROJECT DIFFICULTY METER = 1.5

A sachet is a small perfumed bag. Sachets can be used to make your room or locker smell fresh. If you attach a ribbon, the sachets can hang from a doorknob or from a hook in your locker.

These work great as party favors, but they're fun to make with friends, too! You can supply the cotton balls and the essential oils, which can be purchased in craft stores. Try peppermint, lemon, or lavender to start. These scents are mild and calming.

**You'll Need:**
> fabric pieces
> assorted ribbons or colored twine
> scissors
> cotton balls
> essential oils

1. Cover the work surface with newspaper.
2. Begin with a fabric circle. To make the circle, trace the outline of a dinner plate onto your fabric with a pen and cut along the circle with scissors.
3. Add three to five cotton balls to the center of the circle and pour a few droplets of essential oils on them. Fold the fabric over the scented cotton balls.
4. Seal the fabric by cinching it with a ribbon tied around the opening.

# FRIENDSHIP BRACELETS
## PROJECT DIFFICULTY METER = 3

Create your own bright, colorful jewelry in many patterns and styles. These bracelets are fun symbols of your friendship!

**You'll Need:**
- embroidery floss or craft thread
- tape
- scissors
- optional: beads

1. Look up cool patterns like the fishtail, braid, chevron, and more. Ask guests to share their expertise if they've made friendship bracelets before!
2. Gather around a table.
3. Choose the colors of string you want to use.
4. Knot the strings together, leaving 2 inches of string at the top, and tape those inches to the table.
5. Follow your chosen pattern to create your bracelet.
6. When your bracelet is long enough, tie another knot at the end and tie the two ends of the bracelet together.

# CHAPTER 9

# FOOD FEST

**I**f the kitchen is your favorite room in the house, grab an apron and let's get cooking. Your friends can help you prepare these edible delights, or you can prepare them beforehand for your guests. Make sure to clean the counters and the dishes as you go, and ask an adult to supervise.

## SNACKS

**Veggie plates and fruit platters** are healthy and delicious snack options. Cut up the fruits and veggies and arrange the food on large platters. When it's time to snack, serve the food with small paper plates and napkins. Add a small bowl of yogurt to the center of the fruit platter for dipping. Add a small bowl of hummus, ranch dressing, or onion dip in the center of the vegetable platter for the same purpose.

**Popcorn** is a slumber party staple—especially if you're watching a movie! You and your guests can experiment with fun toppings. Try grated cheese and melted butter, or get really creative and drizzle some chocolate syrup and caramel over the hot popcorn.

Make your own **trail mix** using peanuts, shredded coconut, raisins, pieces of pretzel sticks, and chocolate candies.

Concoct a **sparkling punch**. In a large bowl, mix together seltzer, orange juice, and a container of orange or cherry sherbet. Top with sliced strawberries. Keep replenishing throughout the evening. Yum!

Make an **easy fondue** by melting milk chocolate or dark chocolate chips in a pan over a low heat or in a double boiler until the mixture is smooth. (Let a parent help. It's easy to burn the chocolate.) Allow to cool for a few minutes. Transfer into a bowl.

What to dip in the fondue:

☆ banana slices
☆ cherries
☆ strawberries
☆ pineapple slices
☆ chunks of store-bought pound cake
☆ pretzels
☆ marshmallows

# CHICKEN NACHOS

*Who doesn't love chicken, cheese, and a whole lot
of crunch? This is a great option if you're going for
a sports-themed party.*

**You'll Need:**

cooked rotisserie chicken
(fresh and hot from the
supermarket)

tortilla chips

shredded nacho cheese (usually
a blend of cheddar, Colby,
and Monterey Jack cheeses)

store-bought salsa (use on
the side)

1. Remove and discard the chicken skin, and cut the white-meat chicken into bite-size pieces.

2. Cover the surface of a baking sheet with aluminum foil (for easy cleanup).

3. Spread a layer of tortilla chips over the foil.

4. Arrange some chicken over the chips. Sprinkle cheese over the chicken pieces, and then cover that with more chips. Add one more layer of chicken and then top the whole thing generously with cheese.

5. Bake at 350°F for about 10 minutes or until the cheese is melted.

6. Serve with a bowl of guacamole or your favorite salsa.

# MAKE-YOUR-OWN PIZZA

*Sure, you can order from the local pizza parlor, but this is a delicious and cheap alternative! Plus, it's way more fun.*

**You'll Need:**

premade pizza crust
   (purchased at any local
   grocery store)
canned tomato or pizza sauce
grated mozzarella and
   Parmesan cheese

**Various toppings**

pepperoni slices
cooked spinach
chopped broccoli
cooked hamburger
mushrooms
bell pepper slices
black olives, sliced
diced ham

1. Lay a piece of foil on a flat, working surface. Place the premade pizza crust on top.
2. Have guests spoon tomato or pizza sauce onto the crust and then add cheese and whatever toppings you all would like.
3. Transfer the foil with the pizza on top onto a cookie sheet and bake at 350°F for 10 minutes or until the cheese melts and begins to brown.

# TACO PIES

*Hearty and easy, but be warned—it's got a kick! You'll need an adult helper for this one.*

**You'll Need:**

2 packages of Pillsbury Crescent refrigerated dough

taco filling (makes 4–8 tacos)

1 lb. of lean ground beef

small onion, diced

2 tsp cumin powder

1 tsp chili powder

2 tbsp chopped cilantro

minced clove of garlic

8-oz. can of tomato paste

cooking oil

grated cheese (mozzarella, cheddar, Swiss)

1. In a pan, heat up a few tablespoons of oil and sauté the onion and garlic.
2. Add the meat and the rest of the seasonings. Cook until the meat is no longer pink.
3. Add the tomato paste. Stir. Bring to a simmer.
4. Cover the base and sides of a 9-inch pie plate with triangles from the 2 packages of uncooked crescent dough.
5. Spoon the cooked meat over the dough. Then cover that with a blanket of cheese.
6. Bake at 375°F for about 15 minutes, or until the cheese is melted and the crust is golden.

# BUILD-A-SALAD

*Salad may sound boring, but with the right blend of veggies and toppings, it can be really filling and delicious.*

**You'll Need:**
- romaine lettuce, torn or chopped into bite-size pieces
- diced celery
- shredded carrots
- sliced cucumbers
- cherry tomatoes
- chopped cauliflower
- sliced peppers
- assortment of salad dressings

**Various toppings**
- grated cheese
- sliced hard-boiled eggs
- chunks of cold chicken
- tuna chunks
- croutons
- sunflower seeds
- tortilla strips
- dried cranberries

1. Place each ingredient in its own bowl with a serving spoon.
2. Arrange the bowls on the table, buffet style.
3. Give each guest a bowl and let them build the salad of their dreams!

# S'MORES

*A favorite among Brownies and Girl Scouts, this yummy treat can be made many different ways. Here's a no-brainer recipe that tastes out of this world.*

**You'll Need:**

1 box of graham crackers

6 chocolate bars (or more, if you have more guests!)

1 bag of marshmallows

1. Break a graham cracker in half. On one half, place a square or two of chocolate, and top that with a marshmallow.

2. Cover with the second graham cracker half, and cook in the microwave for about 20 seconds (the marshmallow should puff out, but not explode). Eat.

# FRUITY FUN

*Fruit lovers, unite! This is a kind of fruit compote, and it makes for a refreshing dessert. Ask an adult for help on this one.*

**You'll Need:**

3 cups chopped fruit— peaches, plums, strawberries, and cherries are all great options!

¼ cup water

½ cup sugar

whipped cream

1. Place the fruit, water, and sugar in a large saucepan on low heat.
2. Let simmer for about 15 minutes, stirring occasionally.
3. Remove from heat and let the fruit mixture cool.
4. Pour the fruit mixture into a blender and puree until it is smooth.
5. Spoon the fruit compote into pretty bowls and top with whipped cream.

# TURTLES

*These turtles are yummy chocolate and butterscotch treats.*
*Let your guests take home the leftovers as party favors.*
*You'll need an adult helper for this one.*

**You'll Need:**

2 cups semisweet chocolate chips
2 cups butterscotch chips
12-oz. can of salted cocktail peanuts
5 oz. chow mein noodles

1. Melt the chocolate and butterscotch chips together slowly in a saucepan on a very low heat.

2. When the chocolate and the butterscotch have melted, add the nuts and noodles.

3. Drop by heaping teaspoons onto a cookie sheet lined with waxed paper.

4. Let cool.

5. Store in the fridge in an airtight container. This should make about 5 dozen cookies.

# BERRY CREPES

*Life is berry delicious! Don't let this French name intimidate you. A crepe is just a thin, delicate pancake that's commonly eaten in France. Even if your crepe comes out a little sloppy, it will still taste great. You'll need an adult helper for this one. This recipe makes enough for two crepes.*

**You'll Need:**

1 egg

2 cups plus 2 tbsp low-fat milk

cooking oil spray

sliced strawberries, raspberries, and blueberries

powdered sugar

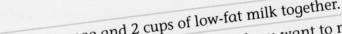

1. Beat an egg and 2 cups of low-fat milk together.
2. Whisk in another 2 tbsp of milk if you want to make the batter thin.
3. Spray a skillet with cooking oil spray and put on the burner on medium heat.
4. Pour the batter into the frying pan in a large circle.
5. Toss a few blueberries, strawberries, and raspberries over the mixture. Cook until small bubbles form. Then, flip and cook the other side for a few minutes.
6. With a big spatula, lift the finished crepe onto a plate.
7. Roll it up, sprinkle with powdered sugar, and add more berries on top.

# STRAWBERRIES-AND-CREAM BISCUITS

*This dreamy dessert doubles for breakfast! If you like things sweet, add a little sugar to the whipped cream.*

**You'll Need:**

ready-made biscuits (or the heat-and-serve kind)

sliced strawberries

fresh whipped cream

1. Pile strawberries and whipped cream in between 2 room-temperature biscuits.

2. Each serving requires 2 biscuits, 2 cups of sliced strawberries, and 2 tablespoons of whipped cream. Yum.

# 10

# GOODIE BAGS AND GOOD-BYE GIFTS

Your slumber party was a huge hit! And now it's time for your guests to go home (and get some much-needed rest!). Give your guests something to remember what a fun time they had. Feel free to give these gifts before, during, or after the party.

## FRUITY LIP GLOSS

*You didn't know you could make your own cosmetics, did you? Make this scent-sational lip gloss and no one will be able to forget your sensational party!*

**For each lip gloss, you need**
> 2 tbsp solid shortening
> 1 tbsp fruit-flavored powdered drink mix
> a small container or jar, empty and thoroughly washed

1. Combine the shortening and the powdered drink mix in a microwave-safe bowl.
2. Place in the microwave on high for about 30 seconds or until it becomes a liquid.
3. Pour the mixture into the containers.
4. Place in the fridge for at least a half hour while the mixture hardens.

# VANILLA SCRUB

*Here's a sweet treat, but it's not for eating!
Tell your guests if they use this scrub in the shower,
their skin will be left feeling smooth as silk and smelling
heavenly. This scrub is for all skin types.*

**For each person, you'll need:**

2 cups kosher salt

2 cups baby oil

1 tbsp vanilla extract

small mason jar

permanent marker, ribbons, and stickers for decoration

1. Mix the ingredients together and pour into individual jars.
2. Decorate the outside of the jar with a label (written in permanent marker), ribbons, and stickers.

## OTHER IDEAS:

☆ Wrap a colorful washcloth and a toothbrush in a little shopping bag and fill the top with colored tissue paper, and there you go! You've got a great goodie bag to give as the party gets underway. You might find this useful if one of your guests forgets something from home!

☆ A pair of cute socks and a few hard candies tossed into a colored cellophane bag is a simple way to say "Thanks for coming to my party!"

☆ Make individual nail kits for each guest. For each, you'll need a nail file, an emery board, some cotton balls, and nail polish. Put the stuff in a gift bag or colored cellophane bag.

☆ A purse-size container filled with sample-size hand and face creams is a neat thing to give your friends. It also ties in nicely with the spa theme.

☆ Wrap several chocolate-butterscotch turtles (see page 89) in a small box or in a plastic bag with a ribbon tied around it. Write the person's name on a sticker, and adhere it to the box or the plastic bag.

☆ How about a bunch of hair ties, headbands, and hair clips wrapped in colored tissue paper and ribbon? This ties in nicely with the glam girl theme.

☆ Give everyone a pair of flip-flops with a large bow tied around the straps.

☆ How about miniature photo albums to hold all the photos you took at the party? Put a photo of the whole group on the front cover.

☆ Bracelets, rings, and other small accessories are gifts that your guests can wear long after the party is over! You can make these or purchase them from a store.

In the morning, you may feel exhausted. But don't worry, you can always take a nap later. Hopefully, you are in a great mood from having the best sleepover party ever!

After breakfast, ask your guests to help you clean up the party room and any other rooms that were used during the party. Your parents will really appreciate this—it shows responsibility and maturity. As your guests' parents start to arrive, help everyone gather their things. Make sure nothing is accidentally left behind. At the door, give your guests a hug and tell them "Thanks for coming!"

The laughs. The stories. The secrets. The games. The dancing. The snacks. The things you made. The memories you now share.

Aren't slumber parties awesome?
Is it time to start planning your next one yet?

# ABOUT THE AUTHOR

JAMIE KYLE McGILLIAN is the author of *The Kids' Money Book* and *Quiz Me*. In addition to being an editor at *Westchester Parent* magazine, Mrs. McGillian teaches four-year-olds. She lives with her husband and two daughters and her pug along the Hudson River. Her home is the site of many sleepovers!

Good night!

**YOU'RE INVITED TO**

_____'S

*Ultimate*

## SLUMBER PARTY

DATE: _____

TIME: _____

ADDRESS: _____

RSVP TO: _____

PLEASE BRING: _____

---

**YOU'RE INVITED TO**

_____'S

*Ultimate*

## SLUMBER PARTY

DATE: _____

TIME: _____

ADDRESS: _____

RSVP TO: _____

PLEASE BRING: _____

---

**YOU'RE INVITED TO**

_____'S

*Ultimate*

## SLUMBER PARTY

DATE: _____

TIME: _____

ADDRESS: _____

RSVP TO: _____

PLEASE BRING: _____

---

**YOU'RE INVITED TO**

_____'S

*Ultimate*

## SLUMBER PARTY

DATE: _____

TIME: _____

ADDRESS: _____

RSVP TO: _____

PLEASE BRING: _____

**YOU'RE INVITED TO**

_____'S

*Ultimate*

**SLUMBER PARTY**

DATE: _____

TIME: _____

ADDRESS: _____

RSVP TO: _____

PLEASE BRING: _____


**YOU'RE INVITED TO**

_____'S

*Ultimate*

**SLUMBER PARTY**

DATE: _____

TIME: _____

ADDRESS: _____

RSVP TO: _____

PLEASE BRING: _____


**YOU'RE INVITED TO**

_____'S

*Ultimate*

**SLUMBER PARTY**

DATE: _____

TIME: _____

ADDRESS: _____

RSVP TO: _____

PLEASE BRING: _____


**YOU'RE INVITED TO**

_____'S

*Ultimate*

**SLUMBER PARTY**

DATE: _____

TIME: _____

ADDRESS: _____

RSVP TO: _____

PLEASE BRING: _____

**YOU'RE INVITED TO**

_____'S

*Ultimate*

**SLUMBER PARTY**

DATE: _____

TIME: _____

ADDRESS: _____

RSVP TO: _____

PLEASE BRING: _____


**YOU'RE INVITED TO**

_____'S

*Ultimate*

**SLUMBER PARTY**

DATE: _____

TIME: _____

ADDRESS: _____

RSVP TO: _____

PLEASE BRING: _____


**YOU'RE INVITED TO**

_____'S

*Ultimate*

**SLUMBER PARTY**

DATE: _____

TIME: _____

ADDRESS: _____

RSVP TO: _____

PLEASE BRING: _____


**YOU'RE INVITED TO**

_____'S

*Ultimate*

**SLUMBER PARTY**

DATE: _____

TIME: _____

ADDRESS: _____

RSVP TO: _____

PLEASE BRING: _____

## YOU'RE INVITED TO

_____'S

### Ultimate
### SLUMBER PARTY

DATE: _____

TIME: _____

ADDRESS: _____

RSVP TO: _____

PLEASE BRING: _____


## YOU'RE INVITED TO

_____'S

### Ultimate
### SLUMBER PARTY

DATE: _____

TIME: _____

ADDRESS: _____

RSVP TO: _____

PLEASE BRING: _____


## YOU'RE INVITED TO

_____'S

### Ultimate
### SLUMBER PARTY

DATE: _____

TIME: _____

ADDRESS: _____

RSVP TO: _____

PLEASE BRING: _____


## YOU'RE INVITED TO

_____'S

### Ultimate
### SLUMBER PARTY

DATE: _____

TIME: _____

ADDRESS: _____

RSVP TO: _____

PLEASE BRING: _____

# PARTY TO-DO LIST!

**Two to Three Weeks Before the Party**

- ❑ Discuss party plans with a parent.
- ❑ Make a guest list.
- ❑ Make invitations and send them out.
- ❑ Plan the menu.
- ❑ Pick the theme and think of decorations to match.

**One Week Before the Party**

- ❑ Buy paper plates, plasticware, and decorations.
- ❑ Write a shopping list for food and drinks.
- ❑ Decide what to put in the goodie bags.
- ❑ Make awesome playlists.
- ❑ Check that all guests have responded.

**Day Before or Day of the Party**

- ❑ Clean the house.
- ❑ Get out your sleeping bag.
- ❑ Shop for the food and drinks.
- ❑ Hang party decorations.
- ❑ Blow up balloons.
- ❑ Make party platters.
- ❑ Pick out an outfit and a pair of cool PJs.
- ❑ Create goodie bags.
- ❑ Run through the games and activities in your head.

# PARTY TO-DO LIST!

**Two to Three Weeks Before the Party**

- ❑ Discuss party plans with a parent.
- ❑ Make a guest list.
- ❑ Make invitations and send them out.
- ❑ Plan the menu.
- ❑ Pick the theme and think of decorations to match.

**One Week Before the Party**

- ❑ Buy paper plates, plasticware, and decorations.
- ❑ Write a shopping list for food and drinks.
- ❑ Decide what to put in the goodie bags.
- ❑ Make awesome playlists.
- ❑ Check that all guests have responded.

**Day Before or Day of the Party**

- ❑ Clean the house.
- ❑ Get out your sleeping bag.
- ❑ Shop for the food and drinks.
- ❑ Hang party decorations.
- ❑ Blow up balloons.
- ❑ Make party platters.
- ❑ Pick out an outfit and a pair of cool PJs.
- ❑ Create goodie bags.
- ❑ Run through the games and activities in your head.

# PARTY TO-DO LIST!

**Two to Three Weeks Before the Party**

- ❏ Discuss party plans with a parent.
- ❏ Make a guest list.
- ❏ Make invitations and send them out.
- ❏ Plan the menu.
- ❏ Pick the theme and think of decorations to match.

**One Week Before the Party**

- ❏ Buy paper plates, plasticware, and decorations.
- ❏ Write a shopping list for food and drinks.
- ❏ Decide what to put in the goodie bags.
- ❏ Make awesome playlists.
- ❏ Check that all guests have responded.

**Day Before or Day of the Party**

- ❏ Clean the house.
- ❏ Get out your sleeping bag.
- ❏ Shop for the food and drinks.
- ❏ Hang party decorations.
- ❏ Blow up balloons.
- ❏ Make party platters.
- ❏ Pick out an outfit and a pair of cool PJs.
- ❏ Create goodie bags.
- ❏ Run through the games and activities in your head.

# PARTY TO-DO LIST!

**Two to Three Weeks Before the Party**

- ❏ Discuss party plans with a parent.
- ❏ Make a guest list.
- ❏ Make invitations and send them out.
- ❏ Plan the menu.
- ❏ Pick the theme and think of decorations to match.

**One Week Before the Party**

- ❏ Buy paper plates, plasticware, and decorations.
- ❏ Write a shopping list for food and drinks.
- ❏ Decide what to put in the goodie bags.
- ❏ Make awesome playlists.
- ❏ Check that all guests have responded.

**Day Before or Day of the Party**

- ❏ Clean the house.
- ❏ Get out your sleeping bag.
- ❏ Shop for the food and drinks.
- ❏ Hang party decorations.
- ❏ Blow up balloons.
- ❏ Make party platters.
- ❏ Pick out an outfit and a pair of cool PJs.
- ❏ Create goodie bags.
- ❏ Run through the games and activities in your head.

## PARTY TO-DO LIST!

**Two to Three Weeks Before the Party**

- ☐ Discuss party plans with a parent.
- ☐ Make a guest list.
- ☐ Make invitations and send them out.
- ☐ Plan the menu.
- ☐ Pick the theme and think of decorations to match.

**One Week Before the Party**

- ☐ Buy paper plates, plasticware, and decorations.
- ☐ Write a shopping list for food and drinks.
- ☐ Decide what to put in the goodie bags.
- ☐ Make awesome playlists.
- ☐ Check that all guests have responded.

**Day Before or Day of the Party**

- ☐ Clean the house.
- ☐ Get out your sleeping bag.
- ☐ Shop for the food and drinks.
- ☐ Hang party decorations.
- ☐ Blow up balloons.
- ☐ Make party platters.
- ☐ Pick out an outfit and a pair of cool PJs.
- ☐ Create goodie bags.
- ☐ Run through the games and activities in your head.

## PARTY TO-DO LIST!

**Two to Three Weeks Before the Party**

- ☐ Discuss party plans with a parent.
- ☐ Make a guest list.
- ☐ Make invitations and send them out.
- ☐ Plan the menu.
- ☐ Pick the theme and think of decorations to match.

**One Week Before the Party**

- ☐ Buy paper plates, plasticware, and decorations.
- ☐ Write a shopping list for food and drinks.
- ☐ Decide what to put in the goodie bags.
- ☐ Make awesome playlists.
- ☐ Check that all guests have responded.

**Day Before or Day of the Party**

- ☐ Clean the house.
- ☐ Get out your sleeping bag.
- ☐ Shop for the food and drinks.
- ☐ Hang party decorations.
- ☐ Blow up balloons.
- ☐ Make party platters.
- ☐ Pick out an outfit and a pair of cool PJs.
- ☐ Create goodie bags.
- ☐ Run through the games and activities in your head.

# PARTY TO-DO LIST!

**Two to Three Weeks Before the Party**

- ❑ Discuss party plans with a parent.
- ❑ Make a guest list.
- ❑ Make invitations and send them out.
- ❑ Plan the menu.
- ❑ Pick the theme and think of decorations to match.

**One Week Before the Party**

- ❑ Buy paper plates, plasticware, and decorations.
- ❑ Write a shopping list for food and drinks.
- ❑ Decide what to put in the goodie bags.
- ❑ Make awesome playlists.
- ❑ Check that all guests have responded.

**Day Before or Day of the Party**

- ❑ Clean the house.
- ❑ Get out your sleeping bag.
- ❑ Shop for the food and drinks.
- ❑ Hang party decorations.
- ❑ Blow up balloons.
- ❑ Make party platters.
- ❑ Pick out an outfit and a pair of cool PJs.
- ❑ Create goodie bags.
- ❑ Run through the games and activities in your head.

# PARTY TO-DO LIST!

**Two to Three Weeks Before the Party**

- ❑ Discuss party plans with a parent.
- ❑ Make a guest list.
- ❑ Make invitations and send them out.
- ❑ Plan the menu.
- ❑ Pick the theme and think of decorations to match.

**One Week Before the Party**

- ❑ Buy paper plates, plasticware, and decorations.
- ❑ Write a shopping list for food and drinks.
- ❑ Decide what to put in the goodie bags.
- ❑ Make awesome playlists.
- ❑ Check that all guests have responded.

**Day Before or Day of the Party**

- ❑ Clean the house.
- ❑ Get out your sleeping bag.
- ❑ Shop for the food and drinks.
- ❑ Hang party decorations.
- ❑ Blow up balloons.
- ❑ Make party platters.
- ❑ Pick out an outfit and a pair of cool PJs.
- ❑ Create goodie bags.
- ❑ Run through the games and activities in your head.

# INDEX